"Lew Vander Meer has written a book ~~...~~ Churchism but might as well be called *The Book of Privities*. This slim book is fat with truths, and as fun to read as fiction. . . . If the goal of a recovering alcoholic is to dry out, the goal of a recovering churchist is to water up. A dried and dusty body of Christ needs to rehab with Jesus at the well and drink again of the Living Waters. . . . I guarantee that you hold in your hand a book that is hard to put down."

  —From the foreword by LEONARD I. SWEET, author of *I Am a Follower: The Way, Truth, and Life of Following Jesus*

"Lew Vander Meer shows how to build a church that is visibly effective, not merely successful. He explains how to implement sound structure that will help any congregation grow spiritually as well as numerically."

  —BILL WILSON, Founder and Senior Pastor, Metro Ministries, Brooklyn, NY

"Every pastor wanting to be a better leader should sit up and take notice. Lew is a seasoned ministry practitioner. *Recovering from Churchism* describes new thinking, creative breakthroughs, and fresh insights based on his own practical experience growing churches while studying the early church."

  —JIM MELLADO, President, Willow Creek Association

"Required reading for all pastors and church leaders! This is an effective, practical, and resourceful book for congregations. If you're serious about church growth in today's postmodern, post-Christian world, this is a must read. Lew will challenge your thinking and give you the tools for a growing ministry in any social setting."

  —DARYL HIGGINS, Senior Minister, First Protestant Church, New Braunfels, Texas.

"Lew Vander Meer has the rare combination of a pastor's heart and a writer's clarity. He writes with a depth and wisdom that make this book a pleasure to read. I recommend it highly."

  —REV. RAY W. BURGESS, UMC chaplain, Tucson, AZ

Recovering *from* Churchism

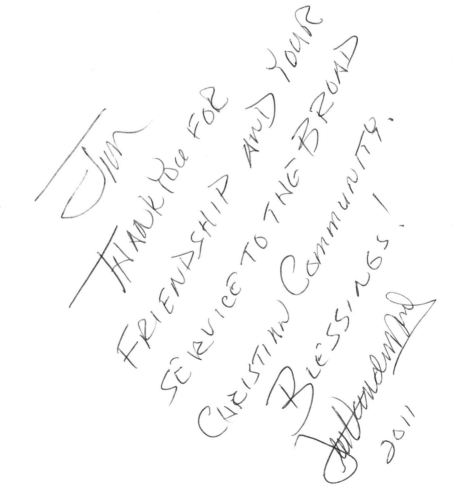

Jim

Thank you for Friendship and your service to the broad Christian Community.

Blessings!

2011

Recovering *from* Churchism

How to Renew, Grow, and Celebrate Your Church

Lew Vander Meer

with
Quentin J. Schultze

foreword by
Leonard I. Sweet

edenridge press

GRAND RAPIDS, MICHIGAN

Published by
Edenridge Press LLC
Grand Rapids, Michigan USA
www.edenridgepress.com
service@edenridgepress.com

Quantity discount pricing is available.
service@edenridgepress.com
Fax: (616) 365-5797

Designed by Matthew Plescher
Edited by Quentin J. Schultze

Vander Meer, Lew
    Recovering from churchism: how to renew, grow, and celebrate your church / Lew Vander Meer ; with Quentin J. Schultze; foreword by Leonard I. Sweet

ISBN 9781937532994 (alk. Paper)
LCCN: 2011939500

REL108010 Religion / Christian Church / Growth
REL108030 Religion / Christian Church / Leadership

Printed in the United States of America

Dedicated to my wife, Alida, and our family for lovingly giving me the time and freedom to immerse myself into the workings of the church; to learn what the biblical church should and should not be.

Acknowledgements

Many members of my church staff and congregation have read and responded to my biblical vision and skills for church growth in today's cultural milieu. I thank all of them.

I especially thank my son and colleague, Mark, and his wife, Mary, for reading early editions of the manuscript and helping to form our shared ministry perspectives and philosophy. Mark's generation of pastors challenged me to be open and honest about the difficulties that prevent many of today's congregations from becoming lively, Spirit-filled churches.

Amy Nattress edited the final copy before sending it on for professional review. She is truly a blessing.

Robert Nattress handled many technical and business matters related to publishing. Without his skills I would still be trying to finish and publish the book.

My entire congregation has been the type of caring church described in this book, believing together that there is a simpler, more biblical and exciting way to "do church." They're the real measure of God's grace in the life of a flourishing congregation. This book is theirs, too.

Long-time friend Quentin Schultze guided the manuscript through the unending details of editing and publishing. His support encouraged me greatly.

Contents

Water Up

When I was growing up in the mountains of West Virginia, a "privy" was a fancy name for an outhouse. I soon learned that the word was etymologically related to "privacy," but because our privy was a two-holer you couldn't even find privacy in the privy. Even when your prayer closet was the earth closet, someone was likely to burst in on you and bring back to earth those high-flying prayers.

It wasn't until my doctoral studies when I was researching the Lollard movement and its founder John Wycliffe, "the Morning Star of the Reformation," that I learned that in the fourteenth century the word was not "privacy" but "privity." In the Wycliffe Bible, privity meant something that was hidden, secret or a mystery, as in Matthew 13:11: "To you it is given for to know the privity of the kingdom of heavens." In medieval times the Book of Revelation was often called "The Book of Privities."

Lew Vander Meer has written a book he calls *Recovering from Churchism* but might as well be called *The Book of Privities*. This slim book is fat with truths, and as fun to read as fiction. But the truths it fleshes out are the hidden truths about God and the church that reveal corruptio optimi pessima: the perversion of the best yields the worst.

Lew's use of "recovering" is payloaded with significance. Alcoholism is an addictive disorder that comes from dependency on artificial substances and stimulation. "Churchism" is also an addictive disorder that comes from dependency on artificial substances and stimulation. Whether or not the church knows it has a problem, and is ready to face its own addictions to hard structures and extracted spirits, is still uncertain. Does the church realize its extent of being a user and abuser of Scripture? Has the church lost the face of Jesus? Has the church lost its healing touch? But there is no better manual for the twelve-step approach to recovery from churchism than this one.

If the goal of a recovering alcoholic is to dry out, the goal of a recovering churchist is to water up. A dried and dusty body of Christ needs to rehab with Jesus at the well and drink again of the Living Waters. Unless we invite the Holy Spirit to "Fill My Cup Lord," and until we find those wellsprings of holiness that are flowing deep and wide, our churchist addictions to artificial substitutes will further disintegrate our dazed discipleship from jocose to bellicose to lachrymose to comatose. "Dem Bones, dem bones, dem..." dried-out bones (Ezekiel 37:1–14) need to Water Up and hear the Word of the Lord. This is a work of profound daring written by a spirit deeply aware of the ultimate cost of truth. I guarantee that you hold in your hand a book that is hard to put down. But once you do, it is hard not to feel a little let down. You will want it to be longer.

—LEONARD I. SWEET

Drew University, George Fox University, sermons.com

Introduction

Chances are your congregation suffers from a debilitating disease. I call it *churchism*. The disease first appeared in ancient big-city churches. More recently, it has infected most denominational congregations. It's even spread to independent and megachurches. Like alcoholism, churchism doesn't respect social class, race, ethnicity, or denominations. It gobbles up congregations in its destructive path.

I know. My name is Lew, and I'm a recovering *churchist*. I've had to surround myself with other recovering churchists for support. We meet in a church. We are the church.

How about you and your church? Do you show any of the following signs?

The Ten Major Signs of Churchism
- Meetings—the more and longer, the better. Churchists rarely see a better solution to any problem and can't imagine a better way of passing time.
- Programs—which must be easily launched and slickly packaged by outside professionals. Churchists believe that for every church activity there must be a prepared program that can facilitate busyness.
- Church policies—which are established or tweaked to dictate congregational behavior. Churchists nip and tuck policies to scuttle whatever they personally dislike.

- Committees—which were, are, and ever more shall be. One of the most cathartic churchist mantras is, "Let's form a committee."
- Fear of adventure—adventure gives churchists angst. Even if the status quo is a dead end, churchists are wary of unique or unusual people and behaviors.
- Professional leaders—who provide top-down management so nearly everything occurring within the walls of the church is under their control. Churchists expect seminary-educated pastors to accomplish all "important" church work.
- Congregational politics—which energize churchists and provide a sense of purpose. Churchists love gossipy conflicts that exercise tongues.
- Membership standards—which effectively keep out of the church those interlopers with baggage, especially sin. Churchists love to surround themselves with people who are just like them so they all can savor their shared righteousness.
- Vacant buildings—which resemble churches, theaters, malls, or supercenter auto lots, but must remain largely empty until Sunday. Churchists appreciate a secure, energy-saving facility that doesn't need to be accessed during the week except by those who print bulletins and policy statements.
- Agendas and minutes—which nicely substitute for a mission statement. Churchists measure congregational progress by the quantity of such minutia stored on the secretary's computer.

Any congregation diagnosed with at least five of these symptoms suffers seriously from churchism. One with seven or more needs acute attention. A church diagnosed with all ten is beyond hope—but for the inexplicable grace of God.

In any case, a churchist congregation can't help itself. The congregation is addicted to unmanageable behaviors. Most sufferers live in denial. They stubbornly believe that working harder at futile tasks will heal them. Only when they admit their addiction can they begin to find real hope with others in recovery.

I know. I grew up in a Christian tradition suffering from churchism. As I describe in the book, I began discerning as an adolescent that although believers loved the Lord they viewed the church as a particular culture rather than as the Lord's own living organism. Well-meaning Christians also assumed that virtually all leadership had to come from the top—the minister, or *domine*—straight down to the congregation. Many men—and they had to be men—didn't want to serve in leadership positions. Church growth occurred by having children and enticing sheep from similar congregations. A legalistic culture firmly held the church together but also prevented growth.

After completing seminary, I began trying to discern a biblical but more culturally flexible approach to governing and growing congregations. I read books, attended conferences, and traversed the thicketed debates over church organization, leadership, and mission. I didn't believe everything the experts claimed because so much of it seemed more about business management than church leadership. Just by asking tough questions, however, I unintentionally became a bit of a renegade in planting, organizing, and growing congregations. I floated new ideas in my own churches. I tried out novel approaches. I delved into church history rather than just accepting the latest programs and popular books. Because I was learning by trying, I made mistakes along the way.

I discovered that churches typically are some of the least innovative organizations in North America. More than that, the most innovative churches frequently are not *biblically* innovative; they copy popular approaches rather than considering Scripture. Christians have the New Testament and two millennia of case studies to learn from. Contrast that with modern corporate management, which has been around for about a century. So why is the managerial approach to leading churches so addictive today? Why isn't there more attention to the biblical and historical records? These are the kinds of questions my restive mind engaged.

After working for decades on developing a more flexible, creative, and biblical way of organizing and leading churches in contemporary culture, I discovered Frank Viola's work on *Reimagining Church: Pursuing the Dream of Organic Christianity.* After studying the apostles, Viola persuasively concluded that Christians today should practice church much like the apostles themselves did in home churches. I agree with Viola's biblical approach. I also appreciate his critique of contemporary church practices in light of early-church practices. I believe that there are normative church practices that "transcend time and culture," to use Viola's language (38). But I'm not convinced that house churches are the best alternative for most congregations.

I first started thinking about the church as "organic" rather than "organizational" decades ago while studying Reformed creeds and confessions. Many of these centuries-old documents talk about the "living" church. They describe the church as a "spiritual organism," as the living body of Christ on earth. Similarly, Craig Van Gelder's *The Ministry of the Missional Church* emphasizes the role of the Spirit in directing how we define and practice congregational life, including church leadership. I discovered in Scripture, historic creeds, and theology the truth that the church is a dynamic, living, body being led by the Spirit. I concluded that the church is called to be both traditional and contemporary in the sense that followers of Jesus Christ are called to live out their historic faith *in their culture*. I suggest in *Recovering from Churchism* that the church itself is *not* merely a culture, but must nevertheless function *in* culture. Every church must express biblical norms through culture.

Churchism develops when Christians become addicted to one formal, cultural way of being and doing church. It can appear in congregations, whole denominations, and even church movements. Churchist congregations became so self-absorbed that even well-intentioned members are ill-equipped to speak faithfully to the wider society and to lead people to Christ. So their congregation either chases after faddish programs or looks to clergy for answers—as if a new minister alone will be able to renew and grow the church. Perhaps it's time once again for churches and denominations to ask themselves honestly if they are equipping people to live faithfully in the world or merely making members dependent on clergy.

Two "G" words—*governance* and *growth*—are intimately related when it comes to leading and nurturing a Christian congregation. I know from experience with a wide range of churches over the last fifty years that the real leaders in many Protestant congregations are not the officials with seminary degrees, impressive titles, and book-lined offices. Great ideas about governing and growing churches often emerge from the humble work of what former Herman Miller CEO Max De Pree calls "roving leaders" who respond quickly and effectively to opportunities (*Leadership is an Art*, 48). How could it be different in an organization formed by the Holy Spirit?

So this book is for:

- Christians who love to *be* and *do* church but who honestly recognize that it's time for their own congregation to try something new or renewed
- Churches that are declining or stagnant—or are growing numerically but still spiritually lifeless, holding little hope

- Congregations divided over how to govern themselves through needed change
- Churches in which some vocal congregants are fearful of new initiatives or simply burned out and therefore uninterested in renewal
- Groups of adventurous believers who are thinking and maybe already praying about planting a congregation and don't want to repeat the same basic procedural mistakes that others have made
- Congregants who desire to make church less political, more enjoyable, and truly glorifying to God

Each of these situations describes persons or congregations that have already recognized that churchism is no longer viable. They've taken the first step toward recovery by identifying their addiction and choosing life over death.

I demonstrate with real examples how to create congregational wineskins for spiritual renewal and growth. I can't promise you a perfect church. I won't guarantee that every last member will love the new, congregation-empowering changes. There will always be those churchists who simply don't like change. But the vast majority of congregants will get on board, invite friends and neighbors to join the renewed congregation, and help make your church a blessed community of service, love, and true Christian ministry. My secret is simply this: I adapt to contemporary culture the approach that the early church used to add daily to their numbers (Acts 2). It works because it's biblical.

Church has to be rejuvenated for every culture in every time and place. Over the years I've reinvented church with congregations as small as a mission chapel and as large as a megachurch with a huge sanctuary-auditorium and acres of parking. I've also served denominational and independent congregations, mentored staff and clergy, and nurtured many intra-congregational and community ministries focused on everything from prayer to addiction recovery, youth, and adult education.

This book is especially for all church leaders—laity and clergy alike—who seek hands-on advice anchored in biblical truth and applicable to different situations, traditions, denominations, demographics, and church positions. Such leaders certainly include committee chairs, pastors, elders, deacons, and everyday volunteers. But the true church leaders are those who envision the future and then make it happen, regardless of what official titles they use and positions they hold. The genuine leaders are those whose Christ-like living and faithful actions demonstrate that they are servants. Unlike the Babylonian leaders who built a tower into the heavens, these true leaders are not trying to make a name for themselves. If you're reading this book, you have already demonstrated that you're a leader. You selflessly aim to serve your congregation. I thank God for you.

I hope that small groups and perhaps even entire congregations will read and discuss this book together to regain their biblical footing and grow richly as faithful, creative followers of Jesus Christ. To our triune God be the glory, now and forever.

1

Celebrating the Church's Unity and Diversity

I love the church—buildings, congregations, worship and even the daily grind of parish work. I grew up in a strong congregation and discovered that I even loved church organization and practice. I loved church the way many entrepreneurs love business and the way many teachers love their students and the whole process of education. I also recognized in my youth and thereafter that the church was not always what it was called to be. I've spent over sixty years watching the church, living in the church, planting churches, and pastoring everything from a small mission chapel to a contemporary megachurch. I believe it's time for me to speak about the church—the vibrant, joyful exciting church. Why? For one thing, I believe I'm called to do so. For another, I love the Lord and the church. I desire to serve others who want to make their church a community of vibrant ministry. Too many congregations are just spinning their wheels.

My childhood congregation was a model of what it was to "be" church in the 1950s: ornate brick, steep front-entry stairs, stained glass windows, wooden pews, chandeliers in the sanctuary, a *domine* (minister) with proper pulpit prestige, and distinguished elders in dark gray suits who shuffled somberly into the sanctuary just before worship began.

In my home congregation, key issues were:

- keeping members away from movie theaters, playing cards, and dancing
- determining whether men could dress informally for the Sunday-evening service (only suits and ties in the morning)
- deciding if ushers (men only) should wear real or imitation carnations in their suit lapels
- finding enough men (and *only* men) to serve as elders
- knowing how to act in the highly unlikely case that a genuine neighborhood visitor actually showed up for worship

My congregation was deeply denominational and held a strict sense of "us vs. them" regarding its relationship to other denominations. Most Christians and congregations were very denominationally sensitive back then. Baptist friends of mine were willing to visit my Calvinist congregation, but stayed seated and silent when we all rose to repeat the Apostles' Creed. At that time, many Protestants viewed Roman Catholics as a cult, and probably vice-versa.

Sociologists tell us that for many decades it was possible to predict the denominational choice of American Christians by their income, among other factors. Calvinists and Episcopalians tended to be middle to upper-middle class, whereas Baptists and Pentecostals generally hailed from the lower-middle and lower classes. Such economic differences fueled separation in the broader church community. Denominations heavily populated with upper-middle and upper-class congregants often would look down on the faith and worship of less affluent believers and denominations. I can still hear wealthy, stoic Calvinists berating Pentecostals and traveling evangelists for being far too emotional.

Tracking Congregational Changes

Much has changed. Megachurches with two-thousand or more participants dot the landscapes near interstate highways. Many upper-class people worship charismatically, expressing plenty of hearty emotion. Many younger Christians don't know traditional hymns but enthusiastically embrace contemporary praise-and-worship music. Projection technology is common in churches of all sizes and most Protestant denominations. Ecumenical worship unites some believers. Newly branded, independent "community" churches are replacing denominational congregations. Alternative worship styles are popping up everywhere, even with traditional churches as separate or blended services. Coffeehouse congregations are growing increasingly common in trendy urban areas.

We're living in the middle of a sea change of church life. But one enduring question remains: how do we best do church? Many Christians today want to hang on to what worked previously, although appropriate change is necessary and pleasing to God. But how and why should churches alter the ways they conduct the Lord's work? Many churches are locked into older practices partly because even just congregational talk of change leads to internal controversies, conflicts, and schisms. This book challenges congregational leaders and other members to look at themselves and their church—and to dare to pour fresh new wine into clean wineskins.

Understanding the Meaning of "Church"

The biblical word for "church" simply means those who are called out of the pagan world of sin and called together to be an assembly of people "in Christ"—the "called out" and the "called together." So when we ask the question of how best to do church, we must realize that we're talking about assemblies of believers who are called out and called together. These are the people asking the question—not social groups, not clubs, not schools, and not neighborhoods. The called out and called together rightly seek to know who they are and how they can actually be who they're supposed to be. Discovering and living such great callings requires a commitment to biblical wisdom, vision, goals, and tasks. We necessarily begin with biblical wisdom.

Capturing the Biblical Basis for the Church

The primary biblical absolute for the called out and called together is *faithfully glorifying God* (1 Cor. 10:31). The second biblical absolute is affirming both the *reality of unity* and the *need for diversity* among all congregations. These are God's own mandates for what his church should be.

Regardless of worship or denominational differences, believers are called together to affirm unity in Jesus as savior and Lord (John 1; John 3; 1 Cor. 1, 3; John 17). Unified in Christ, Jesus' followers celebrate the many dynamic ways congregations and denominations express and implement their distinctness while simultaneously affirming their oneness in Christ. We church members celebrate diversity, recognizing that all congregations can *correctly* express themselves in worship and life without having to do so the exact same ways as other congregations. We celebrate the diversity of people and gifts in the church—the many parts of the one "body." Different ways of doing church are neither right nor wrong as long as they fittingly affirm unity in Christ and gratefully employ their congregants' diversity as congregational stewards. This is the beautiful mystery of the church—a foundation of unity in Christ along with the diversity of congregations, people, and gifts.

Why is this affirmation and celebration of variety within unity important in congregations seeking a fresh look at themselves? Because the church has too often been self-absorbed and excessively critical. Part of a new beginning is the joy of respect, happiness, and positive curiosity as dissimilar people serve alongside one another. Our physical eyes see differences in race, ethnicity, and social class. When we look instead with the eyes of the heart (Eph. 1), we see our shared unity in Christ as the anchor for a shared faith even as we employ our varied gifts.

Understanding the diversity of believers and congregations begins with gratitude, not despair. Before any congregation embarks on its own quest to renew and reorganize itself, it should simply give thanks, celebrating all faithful churches and their congregations, including all faithful denominations and parachurch movements. It's right and fitting for us to celebrate the new wine being poured into new wineskins from church to church, believer to believer. It's biblical for us first to stand with the diversity of people and congregations, joyfully observing all that God is doing. We ought not to begin with paralyzing fear, heart-suffocating negativity, or debilitating conflicts and divisions.

Just like human culture in general, the church today is too diverse and spacious for any one congregation or denomination to capture the work of the Spirit in North America, let alone around the world. The spectacular growth of ethnic churches from coast to coast should itself fill our hearts with delight over what God is accomplishing. A church's problem is not so much whether or not it should embrace new ways of doing church, but instead how to discern which of the many alternatives might be appropriate for each group of faithful believers.

Every summer I rent a huge garden plot in the middle of Grand Rapids, Michigan. I'm surrounded by other renters who farm their plots. What a variety! Black, White, Hispanic, Asian, old, young, male, female, married, single, educated, uneducated. The attorney farms beside the impoverished minority widow, who farms adjacent to the young couple that farms next to the Hispanic entrepreneur. We're all different, yet when we converse, our minds aren't focused primarily on our differences, but on what we share— our seeds, plants, rain, storms, and sometimes even potential thieves. We're focused on the joy of our unity as we seek to grow together. We learn from one another and we delight in each other. We enjoy our diversity because of our common humanity. So it should be with the church. We delight in how God has stitched together a giant, expanding garden quilt out of the patchwork of believers' differences.

The broad church community needs new language: less *they* and *those*, and more *we* and *us*. The first concern when encountering another church or potentially new congregant shouldn't be differences, but unifying gratitude: "In this cruel and faceless world, I'm actually encountering another believer in Jesus—great! Having met this person or been introduced to this congregation, I hope we can learn from one another. Let's have a good time together."

Changing its perceptions and changing its language will help a church see itself as part of the broader church community. The new insight opens the door to a greater willingness to experiment and change. You can have all the methods available to create the new wine and new wineskins, but if the heart of the congregation isn't grateful, methods will fall flat. Rise up with new energy and declare: "We're part of a world of churches, and by grace we will be a unified part of that diverse world!"

Discussion Questions

1. Is your congregation open to discussing change—any change?
2. Have people left your church in the last few years because they wanted more change? If so, what kind of change? Why didn't the church accommodate the change?
3. How would you describe the existing diversity in your church? The existing unity?
4. Is your church leadership open to discussing, considering, or leading change?

2

Casting Your Caring Vision

I was teaching a religion class of Christian high school seniors who were discussing the real and perceived shortcomings of their home congregations. Some students were frustrated because, in their opinion, their church was not reaching more lost souls. As the class talked, I suggested that perhaps all congregations should give up some things to achieve this goal of reaching the lost. One of the complaining students attended a large, classical church of rich heritage. I quipped that perhaps his church give up the fine music and sophisticated liturgy in order to attract the many lower-economic people who lived in the neighborhood. He immediately stated that he could never worship without the classical music and elegant worship. These, he declared, were crucial to true worship.

The young man was making a choice. His church had made the same choice. Is he wrong? Is his church wrong? Is the young man a hypocrite, demanding a necessary ministry goal (evangelism), yet not being willing to sacrifice another area of ministry to get his demand met? Probably not. He's making choices based on his own needs as a believer and what he believes is crucial for his faith and the biblical identity of his church's regular attendees. He's not denying the need for outreach to the lost; he's just realizing that no church can do it all. If he has a true passion for neighborhood evangelism, he may need to find avenues outside of the walls of his classical worship—maybe even switch congregations. Or perhaps he and his congregation need to consider how they might attract potential members from beyond the neighborhood who would be blessed by the same "fine" worship.

Chapter one identified two biblical principles for the church: (1) the church *does everything to the glory of God*, and (2) the church *embraces the diversity of people and gifts within the unity of Christ*. A congregation must embrace these mandates to enjoy the richness of being the church. When a congregation looks at all believers and all churches through the eyes of the heart, its perception shifts from self-centeredness and self-absorption to the excitement of belonging to a diverse, unified group focused on bringing glory to God.

Beholding a Congregational Self-Identity
The absolutes of *glory to God* and *diversity amidst unity* are universal. While embracing these universal absolutes, each congregation must also search out its own, unique identity. This search must be a deliberate act. The church leaders and the members of the congregation must ask questions such as:

- Who are we?
- What is our unique identity?
- What is our unique calling—and our related vision, purpose, and goal?

As your congregation searches for its unique identity, it must realize it can't be and do everything it would like to be and do. Choices must be made. Congregations often feel the pressure to do it all—a myriad of ministries, a plethora of programs. Among the myriad and the plethora, however, the local congregation must deliberately define itself, make fitting decisions, and then live out its unique identity within its choices. A congregation shouldn't beat up itself for failing to do everything the church down the street is doing or not doing, or all the innovative programs the latest church magazine highlights, or not adopting all of the recommendations of the latest church-growth gurus. Each congregation must take pride in doing well what it honestly believes God has distinctively called it to do. A congregation should strive to be great at its own calling rather than simply being mediocre at a host of ill-fitting activities.

The women's neighborhood Bible study. At one congregation, a group of women committed to evangelism met weekly for coffee in the church basement with as many neighborhood women as they were able to bring in. Some of the local women showed interest in the church, and one woman and her family finally showed up for a Sunday morning service. She came once but never returned.

When some women from the church asked her why she never returned, she explained that the mood and character of the weekly coffee gatherings were very different from the mood and character of Sunday worship. The latter, she said, lacked the informality and warmth of the weekly meetings in the basement. Does this mean the church should change how it worships? Perhaps.

The chairman of that church's evangelism committee told me adamantly that doorstep evangelism was sufficient for reaching the lost. "If you lead a person to Christ on the doorstep or in the living room, then the person is saved. The church doesn't need to change itself to draw in people." He declared that a new believer will gradually change and eventually adapt to the congregation's people, practices, and worship. True?

Identifying Your Church's Calling

As a local congregation defines its identity, it must ask what biblical *shoulds* and *musts* will guide its decision-making. The specific shoulds and musts become the congregation's callings. In other words, a specific organization's identity should be what it is called to be and do in its own time and place.

Every Christian congregation knows that its biblical callings include such basics as preaching, teaching, fellowshipping, and evangelizing. When it comes to such essential church practices, the real question for a local congregation is *how* to carry out such biblical demands:

- *How* will we worship?
- *How* will we serve our children and youth?
- *How* will we reach out to the unsaved and unchurched?
- *How* will we care for those we reach out to?

It's the *hows* that that a congregation answers as it defines its unique callings and identity as a congregation. Moreover, how congregations conduct such activities will serve some people more than others. No congregation can be all things to all people. Unless your church is the only one in town, potential members will have choices. They should. God is bigger than any single congregation.

Answering the how questions is difficult. Is the congregation ready to go to a contemporary worship style and risk offending those who love hymns and traditional worship? Are members willing to focus on hymns and traditional worship and risk alienating those who demand edgy creativity? Both worship styles can fittingly fulfill the "praise God" requirement of Scripture. In terms of evangelism, many congregations have proclaimed, "Come as you are; we love you as you are!" When the broken and non-traditional people actually enter the door, however, they find that congregants aren't ready for them. They're loved not as they are, but as they could and should become in the eyes of the church's most active members.

The young couple that doesn't need to worship. A young couple expressed to their pastor their new faith in Christ and their joy of now being in a church. Then they asked if weekday activities in the church could be their worship since they skied and biked most weekends. They went on immediately to tell how they were raised in religious narrowness and negativity and were delighted that this church was so accepting and not judging the way they now were living out their faith. What should a pastor say? How should a congregant who knows them respond?

What the pastor or other congregant tells the couple will probably reflect the basic identity the church has adopted explicitly or implicitly. If the pastor accepts and affirms the couple and later catches heat from congregation leaders and members, clearly divisiveness is forming. If the congregation defines itself in such a way that the couple fits with the congregation, the pastor can defend the church's support of the couple based on the congregation's own definition. Then, even if members object to the couple, the pastor's defense is rooted in the church's identity rather than in one person's opinion.

But the task of defining a congregation's unique identity is often difficult. Personal needs, private tastes, theological perspectives, denominational demands, neighborhood and societal changes, and pressures from special-interest groups all shape identity. Many of these forces compete. The process of defining a unique identity can be filled with tension if not outright conflict.

The senior member who complains rather than leaves. A retired man stood in his urban church's parking lot, declaring that he had grown up in this, "his" church. The urban neighborhood had transitioned and the man had moved to the suburbs. He proudly told of his decision, "My wife and I are staying with the church even though it's a thirty-minute drive each way." He affirmed his church's commitment to neighborhood outreach and declared that his congregation must be mission-minded. He also complained, "The preaching has abandoned the catechism and traditional doctrine in favor of popular topics and the problems of the day." Gesturing toward a noisy group of lower-income minority children running in the church parking lot, he exclaimed, "And something has to be done to keep these hyperactive kids off the property!" If you were a proud member, how would you respond?

Are there right and wrong congregational identities? Probably not—as long as the identity is biblical (God-glorifying, united in Christ, and representing the diversity of people and their gifts), the congregation knows and believes the identity, and its process of establishing the identity is biblical. Any congregants could be the ones to start thinking about and discussing the church's identity, but normally official church leaders must begin the formal process. They must understand that this process is important for the immediate and long-term health and happiness of the church in its own unique time and place.

The process of forming the identity of the congregation usually begins with the pastor, who is sometimes called the "Vision Caster." The pastor has attended seminary and probably is reading books, going to seminars, praying, and thinking about the future of the church. In most cases, the pastor is best equipped to begin casting a vision of what the congregation is being called to become.

Casting a New Church Identity

Casting a vision, though done deliberately, must also be done carefully. Consider two types of casting—casting a rock and casting a fishing lure. Let's say both the rock and the lure are beautiful (at least to a geologist and a fisherman). The rock may be a beautiful rock, but if it's tossed into a spring garden patch, emerging flowers will be broken.

The same is true of the pastor's vision. It may indeed be beautiful. If, however, it's too heavy for the people and is simply thrown at them, the people, like the flowers, may end up broken. The casting should be more like the fisherman and the lure. Cast small pieces at a time, carefully and lovingly, in sermons, Bible study groups, over coffee, and in various meetings. Then, like the fisherman, draw the line back slowly and wait for nibbles. As a pastor casts the vision, the pastor also learns to listen, adjust, and analyze how the congregants feel about a new vision.

As the pastor gains a better sense of the people's thoughts, and as congregants have more opportunities to hear and respond to the vision casting, eventually the time comes to take a more proactive approach. The pastor begins visioning ideas with a few official or unofficial church leaders. *Unofficial leaders* are those who lead simply by their presence and the respect others have for them. The *official leaders* meet regularly to talk, debate, evaluate, react, and critique. The pastor continues to talk and especially to listen to both groups.

After the leaders meet and begin the discussion, the congregation is drawn in: sermons, small-group conversations, questionnaires, congregational meetings, suggestion boxes, discussion in Bible studies and other adult groups, and any other ways the congregation can begin forming and projecting the vision of just *who* this congregation is called to be and how it can uniquely bring glory to God through its diverse people and their many gifts.

It's also possible that vision casting will emerge from within the congregation as members participate in fellowship, study, and worship. This is partly why official and unofficial church leaders at all levels need to be listening to the feedback and ideas being discussed by congregants.

In all of this, the leaders must remember: "We aren't doing this to please the senior pastor or a certain faction of the congregation. We're doing this to be and to further become a faithful, biblical church—the particular church God wants us to be to bring glory to him." If this is the focus and overall goal, much haggling and divisiveness can be avoided—and there can actually be joy in the ongoing discussion and exploration. The process won't always be easy, but it will be biblical. The congregation will realize its callings and begin forming its own identity.

Discussion Questions

1. Does your congregation have a unique vision? If so, how many members know it? If not, what guides the church's ministry into the future? What helps the congregation make decisions about which people to serve or reach out to?
2. Does your congregation have a mission statement? If so, is it written down? If not, do you need one? Can you think of any recent church decisions that could have been addressed better with a vision and/or mission statement?
3. If your congregation sought to change, what aspects would be easiest and most difficult to give up?
4. Has your church been growing? If not, why not? If not, should growth be part of your congregation's vision?

3

Untangling Your Church from Unfriendly Culture

While on vacation years ago, I attended a small country church. The pastor prayed for one of the members who was obviously drifting away from Christ. The proof of this man's drift was that someone from church drove by his house and saw him holding a can of beer. The pastor didn't indicate any drunkenness.

Alcohol is a problem for many people, and congregations ought not to take it lightly. But is drinking a beer necessarily a sign of sin? This church's cultural expression of drinking a can of beer had become its Christian measuring stick. The cultural expression became the church's benchmark of faith. Good idea?

While seeking to bring glory to God by living out its unity and diversity, each congregation searches for its unique identity. Each congregation is called to ask itself some basic questions:

- Who are we?
- What has been our identity?
- How would community people describe us after a visit or two on Sundays?
- What have been our goals?
- Do we need to make some changes?

Doing Church in Culture

As a church searches for its unique identity, it must realize the importance of culture. For example, consuming alcoholic beverages is highly cultural, varying tremendously among people worldwide. Culture plays a huge role in the definition, existence, and life of the church.

"Culture" is simply a word for how people and organizations live. Culture includes how a people works, creates, grows, and changes. Culture is the values and norms (written and unwritten rules) of the people. Culture is what a people considers important and how the laws and traditions of that people protect and promote its values.

Culture itself is neither good nor bad. We're created by God to be co-creators with him of culture—to "cultivate" God's creation as Adam was first called to do in the garden of Eden. Culture can be apostate and evil, denying the influence and presence of God. This was true for the World War II Nazi culture of hate, lust for power, and genocide. Culture can also be God-fearing and good, as seen over and over in the fledgling churches of the New Testament. Many of the founders of the United States unashamedly hammered out a constitutional foundation based on the idea that individual rights, freedom, and democracy would best enable Americans to flourish in their new land. While never perfect, culture can be helpful, valuable, and even beautiful. Culture can be the ways people build cities, create art, form laws, enact justice, teach the young, and care for the less fortunate. Christians are called both to be part of the broader human culture *and* to be uniquely separated from it—to be *in* the world but not *of* the world (Rom. 12:2).

The specifics of culture will change from place to place in the world. Some basic practices such as nurturing children and being faithful in marriage are widely valued. The unique ways that even such universal values and practices are expressed and enforced, however, will differ considerably from one nation or group to another. All cultures seem to believe in some form of faithfulness and boundaries in marriage, for instance, while cultures might differ on specifics such as corporal child discipline and birth control.

Recognizing Your Church's Cultural Roots

Even within the same culture there are *subcultures* (cultural variations within larger cultures). All parents in a middle-class American community might value the dignity and happiness of their children. But some families might seek these goals extensively through art and education while others may stress sports or hard work.

Culture should be important to the church. In one sense, the biblical mandate for the church is to create God-glorifying culture through unity and diversity. How do we achieve that mandate culturally? In terms of music, one congregation will faithfully glorify God through Bach and Handel, another through southern gospel and bluegrass, another through hymns from the nineteenth and twentieth centuries, and still another through the kinds of contemporary religious music heard on religious radio. All of these churches seek to establish a church culture that glorifies God. They just "cultivate" differently.

As I explained above, culture itself—as a human calling to develop God's creation in every area of life—is neither good nor bad. No one type of music necessarily glorifies God better than the others. When Russian churches faithfully glorify God, they generally use Russian music, graphic art, architecture, and clerical robes; Africans express God's glory through African culture(s); Jamaicans through Jamaican culture(s); Canadians through Canadian culture(s); and so on.

The question for your church is how its congregants' cultures have or should shape the way the congregation does church. The congregation I was raised in was formed out of a Dutch culture almost directly from the Netherlands. That ethnic past shaped how members received proper unity and diversity. The congregation's own implicit identity was that of a Dutch-American, Calvinist group culture.

Eyeing North American Cultures

When Americans faithfully glorify God, they use one or another part of American culture as shaped by its many ethnic, racial, and religious groups. In a continent as varied as North America, what exactly *is* culture? How does the church express glory to God using American or Canadian music? What is North American music—jazz, swing, blue grass, rock 'n roll, or ...? What about Canada's First Nations? All of these variations reflect "North American" culture, yet some, all, or none may well be how a particular American congregation is called to faithfully glorify God.

Here is where things get sticky. The process of creating, maintaining, and changing *cultures* (entire ways of life) is a gift from God, and an avenue for expressing our values and beliefs, which themselves can be very good or bad, right or wrong, fitting or inappropriate. If a particular congregant or a congregation doesn't like a certain cultural expression, they might label it bad or evil or unbiblical even though the Bible says nothing specifically about it. Examples include rock 'n roll music, artificial insemination, and cremation.

Distinguishing Between Taste and Truth

When a congregation or a particular Christian doesn't like something in culture and finds it repulsive, but there's no specific mention in the Bible, does that thing or action necessarily become evil and unbiblical? Or are we simply talking about matters of taste, preference, or appropriateness? There was a time when pianos and organs were not part of many North American church cultures. Another time, guitars were excluded. Were organs and guitars unbiblical at one time and then later became biblical? Is hard-core rock music with wailing guitars and beating drums simply a matter of taste or is there something uniquely biblical or unbiblical about its use in worship?

Culture often is considered biblical or unbiblical based on personal or group taste. Congregations simply assume that one cultural preference is more faithful than others—or they search out biblical passages just to endorse or condemn their existing preferences. Christians who insist on wearing formal clothing to worship might point to biblical passages on God's glory and coming into his presence with praise. Those who dress informally for worship point to Jesus' words about worship being "in Spirit and in truth." Thankfully, such disagreements are usually friendly.

Inscripturating Culture

Sometimes, though, congregations will *inscripturate* a cultural thing, expression, or activity—elevating it to the level of Scripture. They transform a cultural thing or practice into an end in itself; culture *becomes* true faith instead of being one *expression* of true faith. This helps us to understand why a church might create laws, rules, and rituals that aren't explicitly in the Bible. Inscripturating culture becomes a way to test a person's relationship with Jesus Christ. Churches inscripturate culture when they take strong, inflexible, dogmatic stands on such practices as Sunday (Sabbath) activities, use of alcohol, hair and dress styles, methods of child-rearing, and more. This isn't to say these practices aren't important—the point is that culture rather than biblical insight can become *the* test for a person's faith in Jesus. When this happens, a church's own identity is tied to a particular culture.

Consider Roman Catholic's use of Bingo for fundraising. Protestants have often criticized Catholics' spirituality because of such "gambling." Meanwhile, many upper-middle-class Protestants eagerly invest in stocks and real estate, taking great financial risks in the hope of making money. A Protestant argues that such practices aren't gambling since one is investing—i.e., buying actual products. The debate goes on—whether Bingo and investing are really gambling, and how faithful a person is who engages in such activities. But the Bible never talks about gambling, and certainly not about stocks and Bingo. Yet these practices have been a significant part of spiritual discussions and congregational identities within some cultures.

Another example is worship style. Scripture doesn't specifically define how we're to worship. Here again, cultural expressions—which are appropriate and necessary in and of themselves—have often become "bible." This is seen in the example of quiet versus noisy worship. Most traditional churches provide a quiet sanctuary prior to worship and will defend it by quoting a passage such as "Be still, and know that I am God" (Ps. 46:10). They may even hang a sign above the sanctuary entry doors informing people to proceed silently. By contrast, contemporary worship venues often are noisy, with people walking around, talking, and drinking coffee. A loud video plays on a projection screen or a band rehearses. Contemporary worshipers will defend their biblical right to "make a joyful noise to the Lord."

The quiet people may criticize the noisy people, using God and the Bible as the basis for the criticism. They might say, "God doesn't want us to act noisily before worship." The Bible, however, doesn't specifically describe worship sound. Yet each culture tends to define and defend its own ways of worship.

Culture: the way we live. Culture: our values and how we express them and live them. Culture: God's wonderful gift to society in general and his church in particular. With the great gift of culture comes the variety churches. Yet with culture comes people who begin criticizing other cultures—fairly or not.

Separating Inner and Outer Faith

God's church must learn to distinguish between the inner value (faith and what the Word truly says) and the external, cultural expression. If we judge the quality and reality of the inner value by the cultural expression, we risk

God's disapproval (Matt. 7:1). We also risk losing the beauty of church unity and the joy of congregational diversity (1 Sam.).

Jesus addresses this beautifully in his Sermon on the Mount (Matt. 5–7), delving into the inner being, the heart. He condemns the practice of basing faith and the quality of faith only on the external expression, the observance of the law. Jesus demands that we plumb the depths of our hearts. What is our motivation for the deed, for our cultural practices? Are our hearts truly broken for God and people? Do we strive to go beyond accepted church culture and constantly look for new and significant ways to care about people and faithfully praise God? Only when we see behind the immediate culture and enjoy people's inner faith will the church and all congregations experience true unity and celebrate each other's diversity. Then, God will really be glorified.

Discussion Questions

1. How would you describe your church's culture?
2. How would you describe the culture(s) in the community near the church? Is it the same as the congregation's culture? Why or why not?
3. What parts of your church's worship are matters of taste or style? Are the leaders and congregation open to reconsidering worship style?
4. How did your own family inscripturate culture when you were growing up? As a follower of Jesus Christ, do you still affirm your childhood culture? Explain.

4

Challenging Churchism

One of my own congregations faced a challenge when we decided that one of our callings was to assimilate "returning citizens" (the name chosen by the Michigan Department of Corrections for those recently released from prison to be re-integrated into society). We began with the belief that we could glorify God by being open to this needy segment of the population. Such a decision demanded that we look at who we were and what we would need to do and become in order to serve them.

We also knew that it was unrealistic to simply open the church doors and say, "Anybody and everybody is welcome and nothing about you matters—we all love everybody!" There had to be boundaries. What about criminal sexual offenders? What about those imprisoned for murder and violence against family members? We knew we couldn't simply adopt an "anything goes" attitude.

Such an adventure in congregational change raises significant questions. What can and must change? How do we educate the congregation? How do we guarantee that those in the church who strongly support this change don't turn off the majority of people who have reservations? How do we deal with members' disappointment if some newcomers from the prisons revert to their old lives and perhaps even must be reincarcerated? How do we best incorporate the successful returning citizens into the daily activities of the church? We had many questions for ourselves even as we felt called to serve "ex-offenders" by inviting them into our church culture. The real issue was how we would have to change our own church culture to serve those from outside our culture. How much of our comfortable churchism would we have to give up?

Gender Roles As Cultural Constructs

One example of cultural change within church is gender roles. In early North America, the male did the heavy, intensely physical labor: plowing, digging, baling, hunting, and hauling home the fruit of the hunt. This labor was heavy, intense, and accomplished away from the house. A wife necessarily had to focus on homemaking and caring for the children. There were no perceived options. These were specific roles for the man and the woman. The man had to make the "big" decisions related to hunting, farming, moving to a new farming location, and protecting the family from enemies. Men used guns to guard the house and farm, and to hunt down cattle thieves. Women had to tend to the "simple" tasks and decisions of childcare and cooking.

When it came time in the early church to interpret Scripture's designation of husbands as "heads" of the family, interpretations fell in line with the culture of that era (Eph. 5:21–33). Obviously the man was the leader, protector, and primary decision maker regarding his family's well-being and safety. Headship, then, was identified with leaving the house each morning, being the strong leader and defender, and guiding the family through the wider social wilderness.

This cultural idea of male and female roles was planted in the mindsets of many European and American generations. As Western society moved past the 1960s, the culture of male and female roles changed in the broader society, but often not in the church. Today many Christians still cling to cultural ideas that the man must have the last word, make the big decisions, and guide the family through the wilderness while the woman quietly cares for the house and the children. The husband often assumes he has the freedom to wander (athletic teams, fishing trips, working overtime), while the wife remains home. When the husband stays home with the children, he often tells his friends he must "babysit."

Today, it's generally a couple's personal choice to think and live this way. It's one cultural option. But what happens when this picture of gender and marriage is presented as *the* way to think and live if you really love God and are faithful to his Word? Are such gender roles the Words of God or the words of culture?

Suppose a congregation sends a message to a couple that has somewhat reversed these traditional roles that the pair is living unbiblically. Imagine a church that assumes if a husband stays home to care for the children he is violating the will and Word of God, and that the working wife is disobedient. Is that congregation projecting the true will of God or a "scripture" of culture? Has culture become inscripturated? The will of God is critically important. But so is a congregation's responsibility to ensure that cultural patterns aren't themselves mistaken for the will of God. Moreover, this is just as true for how the church is organized and run as for what it officially or unofficially claims to believe.

Willing within Culture

The power of culture can also impede one's personal will. When a person becomes a Christian they're given a new heart with a new nature (Eph. 4; Col. 3). Romans 6 says all believers inherit a new life with Christ. "I no longer live," says the apostle Paul, "but Christ lives in me" (Gal. 2:20). Romans 8 teaches about the new mind, the mind of the Spirit. Philippians 2 tells the believer to have the mind of Christ. The apostle Peter urges holiness as Christians are "living stones" being built into a "spiritual house to be a holy priesthood" (1 Peter 2:5).

Regardless of culture, our new nature lives! Our new human will is real—in Christ. Like all believers, I must live the new life, affirm my new will, and no longer follow the mind and ways of the world (Rom. 12:1, 2). I must not fall back into the old ways, especially the prevailing ways of the world (this is a theme of the book of Hebrews). Rather, I should confidently expect God to lead, guide, and renew me from the inside out for daily living. God speaks to me by his Word and Spirit, and I'm expected to live that will of God and to reveal it to others. But I will be faithfully expressing this new mind, self, and will through the culture in which I live.

I can't be human let alone faithful without culture. In fact, I can't live outside of my culture. My culture will be the vehicle through which I more or less faithfully live my new life. When does that culture interfere with my new heart, mind, and life so that I and others will need to re-create it or form an alternate culture? At what point does my familiarity with the cultural patterns I adopted *become* what I naïvely begin to believe are the *only* ways to faithfully live my new life?

Avoiding Ethnocentrism

One way we inscripturate culture is *ethnocentrism*. Ethnocentrism is the belief that "my group is the best"—my race, ethnicity, background, habits, or tradition is the superior way to live. An elderly woman from the Midwest returned from an overseas trip during which she spent time in a bustling New York international airport. She remarked about the many "strange" people she saw there. Strange? Or simply different from her? Humans tend to ethnocentrically assume that their culture is normal and everyone else's culture is odd. This becomes a spiritual problem when members of a church assume their way of doing church is *the* normal or biblical way—and all other ways are wrong.

There is some social value in ethnocentrism. Ethnocentrism creates a sense of group identity with all the warmth, identity, and connectedness associated with a small-group feeling. The spiritual problem arises when such feelings and identity oblige everyone else to live and worship similarly. An ethnocentric church feels warm and secure. Everyone knows how to act. It's the safe culture, the right culture, the correct culture, and presumably the biblical culture. The thought of reshaping this culture so it is more appealing to outsiders is discomforting, even threatening. The invitation on the church sign reads, "Come as you are—all are welcome." What happens when the congregation realizes it needs to adjust its culture to effectively minister to those dwelling outside its doors?

Practicing Multicultural Hospitality

A congregation is called to fulfill the biblical mandate to glorify God. But how does the church do that in a multicultural community? The place to begin is not to fret about cultural change, but to discern what the Bible actually says. The inspired, infallible Word of God must be at the center of every church and its decisions. Each church must always ask, "Is what we're demanding of others truly the Word of God or have we merely elevated our culture to the level of God's Word?" If we are to hospitably encounter other cultures, we must get past our ethnocentrism and be open to "different" people and new ways of doing church.

Of course not all cultural change is right and fitting. Some change could be wrong for the church. It could lead existing members away from Christ. It could violate God's commands. But change could also lead the church to a more biblical, Christ-centered, hospitable way to express and live the faith.

If we're committed to unity in diversity as we glorify God, and if we together seek biblical discernment, we will become a more biblical as well as a more hospitable church. This is the exciting journey of faith in the midst of dynamic cultural changes. It might seem utterly confusing at first because its results are unpredictable. Reconsidering our church's culture is also an opportunity to discern how to better bless others and to be more fully blessed. A faithful congregation avoids merely inscripturating culture and instead seeks to live out a truly biblical faith in the midst of the very cultures in which it finds itself.

Discussion Questions

1. Has your church welcomed and worked with new and perhaps unique people? If so, did things work out or was the congregation disappointed? What really happened—and does it say more about the congregation or the new and unique persons?
2. How does your congregation think about gender? How does it act toward male or female visitors? Single or married visitors?
3. Is your congregation economically and culturally diverse? If so, why? If not, why not? If not, how is your congregation diverse?
4. What does your congregation presently do to make visitors feel at home? Explain why the efforts are successful or not—and how you might do this more successfully.

5

Admitting Your Current Messages to Outsiders

A woman who started attending our church told me she was looking for a new spiritual home. The church she was attending would not permit her to be a door greeter because she smoked cigarettes. Similarly, a devout Christian man told me he was not permitted to sing at a nursing home because he had too many tattoos. Interesting dynamics occur when unique people encounter the church—and when the church encounters other cultures and subcultures.

When a church uncritically inscripturates culture, it makes itself less hospitable to visitors and others inquiring about the church. A new person naturally wonders, "Will I violate this group's cultural norms? What will they expect of me? Will I be rejected?"

Accepting Your Church's Own Outsiders

Challenges to existing church culture also emerge from within congregations. What if a member of the congregation hears a different voice of the Spirit and feels called to an unconventional life and faith expression? What if this person in the congregation challenges the comfort zone of the congregation? This challenge could be such things as theology, lifestyle, diet, enthusiasm for evangelism, and clothing styles.

What would your church assume about the following "outsiders":

- the young musician who wants his jazz band to play for the morning service
- the single woman who wants to become a mother through medical procedures
- the unshaven guy in shorts and a backwards baseball cap who always arrives late for worship, carrying his gas station coffee mug
- the newly-on-fire-for-the-Lord believer who wants to be baptized through total immersion even though as a child he was baptized by sprinkling, but now doesn't consider that childhood baptism legitimate
- the inspired artist who wants to hang a highly distinctive and unusual banner in the sanctuary

Would there be room for such people in your congregation? Room for what they want to do? Room for not just words of acceptance, but for a true enfolding of them into your faith community?

On a purely cultural level, a unique person and the congregation won't intimately connect. If the congregation can't accept those aspects of alternate cultures that are not forbidden by Scripture, the church will reject nonconforming persons who might leave the church and even be lost to Jesus Christ, especially if there aren't other accommodating congregations.

Rejecting Monoculturalism

When unique people either leave or never join the church, the congregation eventually becomes monocultural. Most of the people will look and think the same. Their claim to outreach and church growth will primarily be sending money to foreign missions. They might recruit new members who are just like them—especially from other, similar churches. But they will bring distinctive people into fellowship with Christ and the congregation only as long as the saved outsiders remain thousands of miles away.

Worse yet, monocultural congregations tend toward pride. The congregation will congratulate itself on its purity, stability, and spiritual strength. The surrounding community, however, may see the congregation as prudish, self absorbed, and arrogant—if not self righteous. The congregation won't be known for its love of Jesus as much as for its lofty self regard.

Admitting Congregational Stigmas

A self-focused congregation also risks creating the stigma of a negative public image. This happens through the *fallacy of composition* and the *fallacy of division*. We humans tend to view an organization based solely on our knowledge of and relationship to one individual from that organization. We assume that the organization is composed of everyone like the sole person we know. Conversely, the public reputation of an organization such as a church leads outsiders to think that any individual from the organization is just like everyone else in that one church.

For example, suppose I get to know a fellow college student from Bent Forks Fellowship Church. This student rarely studies and frequently parties. Although I know nothing about the person's church, I begin to think of Bent Forks as a liberal congregation that doesn't faithfully nurture its youth. Now turn the example around. Everyone supposedly knows that Bent Forks Fellowship is a liberal church that doesn't care about raising its children in the Lord. Meeting a student who is a member of that church, I immediately assume they're probably not a real, dedicated Christian.

Or suppose I work with a person who is cold, critical, and unloving. He tells me he's from Friendly Church down the street. I conclude that Friendly Church is cold, critical, and unloving. Conversely, Friendly Church has a reputation for being cold, critical, and unloving. I meet someone at work who tells me they're from Friendly Church. I conclude that my coworker is cold, critical, and unloving. According to my "division," Friendly Church is not the kind of place I want to visit—regardless of what the congregation calls itself.

Even though these are fallacies, the power of perception is still at work. This is how the human mind often processes cultural and individual differences. The actions of one member become the identity of their church (*composition*), while the reputation of the church becomes the identity of the sole member (*division*).

Listening to Your Church's Public Messages

All congregants need to ask themselves at least two critical questions. First, "What message am I sending to the world about my church?" As people get to know me and discover that I attend a particular church, what do they conclude about the nature of my church? Second, "What message is my church sending to the outside world?" When people hear that I attend a certain church, what feelings do they have about me? Believe it or not, churches' primary public identities are based on the good or bad gossip about them. Word of mouth is more important than advertising, such as fancy church displays with clever messages. Such signage sometimes creates the impression that the congregation itself is a joke.

Pondering the Early Church's Identity

Just after Pentecost in the early church, all kinds of different people worshiped together and loved each other: rich, poor, slaves, slave owners, educated, uneducated, and Jewish and Gentile (Acts 2:42–47). Sometimes there were relational problems, including self-serving pastor-preachers (1 Cor.). Church history tells us that in spite of these issues, however, the boldness of the faith and the threat of persecution bonded people together. Christians were often scorned, sometimes because of non-Christians' misunderstandings. But Christians were also admired because they loved outsiders as well as insiders. They were eager to bring the Gospel to kings and queens, yet also willing to walk out their front doors and minister to those dying of the plague. This cross-cultural love led many to be added daily to their number (Acts 2:47).

Jesus compares the Kingdom of God to a mustard seed which grows to be a huge tree in which birds make their nests (Luke 13: 18–19). God's kingdom is vast. In a sense, the Kingdom of God is also the local congregation. The local church needs to provide space in its branches for many different birds, even strange species and injured ones that need a place to rest and nest.

Capturing a True Congregational Identity

Christ—not any single culture—must be the true unifying power in a congregation. If Christ is the unity, then Christ's love will characterize the congregation and its individual members. The church will be diverse, yet unified. The church will be known by its unity as well as its diversity. It will be known for loving and accepting people. The people in the wider community who are identified with that church will be known by their love (John 13:35)—just as Christ lovingly calls everyone to himself. That congregation may not be equally hospitable to everyone since it will still bear the marks of its own culture. But if its internal culture is marked by loving inclusion rather than arrogant exclusion, the congregation will, in its own, limited ways, broaden the diversity of its membership in tune with the early church.

What if a visitor seeks membership but lives a life the congregation disapproves of? Should a church want such a person to become part of its public identity? That's an important question! What identity should a church want? Monocultural? Or would it be biblically adventuresome to be known as the church that accepts the unchurched? This could be risky, but it also could create a whole new reputation.

Of course, churches must practice biblical discernment. There are biblical boundaries that should determine who is and who isn't in the church of Jesus Christ. There are biblical boundaries for the lifestyles of God's people. Nevertheless, we must be sure that the boundaries employed by our own congregation are deeply biblical and not just superficially cultural—that we as a congregation are not simply affirming our own relatively monocultural, inscripturated culture. How ready is your congregation to be diverse? How ready is your congregation to be unified by faith in Jesus rather than its ingrown culture?

Discussion Questions

1. Are there unique people in your congregation who have opportunities to express themselves—and do others care to listen? Why or why not?
2. How would members of the surrounding community describe your church and congregation? How do you know? If you don't know, how would you find out? Does it make any difference to you?
3. Does your congregation ever hear about—perhaps in sermons, educational sessions, coffee confabs, and the like—specific examples of things that occur which reflect on how your church is viewed in the community? If so, what do those examples say about you? If not, why not—and how might you collect and share such examples?
4. How difficult would it be for your congregation to warmly accept into membership someone who lives a different lifestyle—maybe even just dresses differently? What types of lifestyles would or would not be acceptable to most existing church members—and why?

6

Serving People Rather than Institutions

An elderly couple moves into a condo near the church. They begin attending the church and get to know the pastor and many congregants. One day the couple announces to the pastor that although they're not married, they urgently desire—in response to a recent sermon series on marriage—to be wed. They also declare how happy they are in the church, that they have come close to the Lord, and that they really enjoy the "Over 70" group.

Much to the couple's surprise, their request is denied. It will take many weeks to complete the pre-marriage classes and they must move apart from each other during that time. Disgruntled, they leave the church and never marry. Was that an example of excellent, caring ministry? What vision of the church is reflected in such a decision? What does the decision say about the church's identity?

I've suggested that if the church is to escape inscripturated culture, prideful ethnocentrism, and a negative public identity, it must commit to the biblical mandate of faithfully glorifying God. But it's a big jump from "faithfully glorifying God" to a healthy understanding of the church's relationship to culture. How can a church move from the goal of faithfully glorifying God to a biblical understanding of itself and its callings? The answer is that the church should focus on *caring for people*.

Loving God and Neighbor As Self

One of Jesus' best-known commandments to early believers is that his followers should love God, first, and then their neighbor, second—as they love themselves (Matt. 22:36–40). This was Jesus' summary of the law and the prophets. It is essential for a person's faithful heart and action.

Already in the Garden of Eden, "God saw it was not good for man to be alone" (Gen. 2:18). Immediately after creating the world and humankind, God focused on his own "vertical" relationship with people, followed by humans' "horizontal" relationships with one another. Whether it's the prophet Elijah or Jesus' daily ministry, the Bible's stories illustrate that people's relationships with God shape their relationships with one another—and vice versa. People are scolded, punished, saved, healed, fed, taught, delivered, and lifted up—by God and one another. Jesus tells us that faith's cutting edge between now and heaven is for his followers to care selflessly for people (Matt. 25). James says that true religion is caring for widows and orphans (1:27). Jesus himself came to earth to be a servant to his people (Phil. 2:7). Jesus invites people to come and eat with him (Rev. 3). When the apostle Peter's relationship with Jesus is restored, Jesus tells him to feed the Lord's sheep—God's people (John 21:17).

A faithful church must envision how it will care for people in Jesus' name. Broadly speaking, a faithful congregation must envision how it will translate its *vertical* love of God into its *horizontal* love of people. Proverbs 29:18 warns against a lack of *vision* (revelation from God). Since the Bible focuses on the church's role of caring for (or ministering to) people, *a church's working vision is caring faithfully for people in order to glorify God as a diverse (multi-gifted and called) but unified (in Christ) body of believers.*

With this working vision, people are the object of service, just as Jesus is the object of glorification; we glorify God partly by caring faithfully for people. This is the picture of the church in Acts 2. Starting at verse 42, the church eats together, learns together, worships together, prays together, socializes together, and takes care of peoples' needs together. Worship and service go hand in hand. Because of their gratitude to God, their love of Jesus, and their openness to the Spirit, Jesus' followers gratefully cared for one another. Life itself became a kind of worship—or at least an extension of assembled worship. As I will explain, such service includes proclaiming the Gospel and bringing lost people into relationship with Jesus and the church. In other words, the church's care for people is meant to be *holistic*—mind, body, heart, and spirit.

Calling all Gifts

Caring for people is a huge venture. There are so many people, so many needs, so many specific ways to care. Each church needs to identify which people it has the passion and means—the calling and related gifts—to serve. Caring is service; we care for others by serving them. A congregation's identity and calling will be shaped by *who* will be served and *how* they will be served. The *who* defines the people being served. The *how* defines the means—the church in action. Taken together, the *who* and *how* for each congregation become its mission statement. The mission statement realizes the congregation's vision by integrating its God-given identity and its Spirit-directed desires. In other words, the church's *mission statement specifies who the called-together congregation is, who specifically is called to serve, and how specifically it intends to serve those people.*

Taken together, a congregation's *whos* and *hows* will be its *goals* and *tasks*. All churches will, of course, care for their own congregants as well as visitors. In addition, congregations will determine how to reach the people God has placed nearby. Rural congregations may want to focus on the plight of poor farmers. Inner-city congregations might care for the homeless or unemployed. Suburban congregations might reach out to workaholic couples and spoiled youth. Urban congregations may want to look carefully at teen ministries in the face of broken families and youth gangs that sometimes serve as surrogate families. These are only a few examples of possible forms of outreach that churches might develop as they specify the *whos* and *hows* within the working vision of caring for people.

Each church, then, has the following:

- **a biblical mandate**—heeding the call out of the world and into fellowship in order to *glorify God* as a diverse (various people with different gifts) and unified (in Christ) body of followers of Jesus
- **a working vision**—*caring* for people holistically (body, mind, heart, and spirit)
- **goals**—*who* specifically you are called and gifted to care for
- **tasks**—*how* you will care for those you are called and gifted to serve
- **a mission statement**—a succinct expression of the congregation's own specific identity, goals, and tasks

Will the focus on serving people minimize the importance of doctrine and solid worship? Actually, the opposite should be true. Correct and thorough doctrine and solid worship become keys to holistic serving. You can't care about people's education and maturation without teaching them a body of correct knowledge (*doctrine*). Solid classroom teaching and pulpit preaching are essential for fulfilling the working vision of caring for people. The same is true for worship. People won't be drawn into the church and continue to come back without solid, biblical worship. Moreover, without such worship members will be far less likely to see the rest of their lives as worship—as means for glorifying God.

Yet in order to fulfill its mission statement, a church must nurture doctrine and worship in ways that truly address people's needs. Worship and teaching need to be relevant and challenging. Good doctrine and some form of biblical worship aren't enough. Suppose a pastor teaches from Genesis 3 that Eden is the scene of the first (original) sin. The pastor explains humans' "fallen" (sinful) nature using Romans 1 and 5. But now what? The pastor then reminds congregants of their sin and calls them to repent. These are great words—*sin* and *repentance*—but how do they connect with contemporary cultures? With congregants' everyday lives? This is the hard work. Drawing general doctrine from theological books is considerably easier than applying it in service of others.

Finding ways to link biblical doctrine to people so they're gripped, moved, and motivated to return next week is the tough task. For example, a congregant wants to know how the reality of the Fall and of sin speak to their own situation. What about divorce, abuse, unemployment, and broken relationships? Then the relevancy of sin must be communicated with an effective delivery and a heart of compassion. Finally, every sermon should frame contemporary culture in the Good News of salvation through Christ. Human brokenness is never the end of the biblical story of grace. When a pastor achieves such goals, people will return for more sermons and for fellowship, education, and eventually to learn how to serve others.

Striving for Excellence

A sermon satisfying the above criteria is an illustration of an overriding principle regarding how well a church should serve people—what the apostle Paul calls "a more excellent way" (1 Cor. 12:31). In congregational ministry, excellence breeds excellence. Excellent preaching inspires excellence in all congregational activities. Excellent preaching requires solid teaching and relevant application. In worship, excellence includes the quality of the delivery of the message; the quality of the playing of the music; the quality of the organization and flow of the worship service; the skillful abilities of the worship leaders to communicate lyrics; the cleanliness, convenience, accessibility, and navigability of the grounds, building, and worship space. By attending well to such matters, a church cares excellently for visitors and members alike. I'm using the phrase "caring for" to capture both the "for" and the "about" of holistic caring.

In *Here I Am: Now What on Earth Should I Be Doing?*, my colleague Quentin Schultze says that the biblical concept of caretaking includes both caring *for* and caring *about* (50–51). Caring "about" others is heartfelt compassion. Caring "for" others is excellence in the caring tasks—in such caring tasks as counseling, teaching, mentoring, preaching, leading, listening, and so on. Schultze says that Christians tend to emphasize one or the other aspect of caring rather than integrating the two into holistic service to church and career alike.

Caring excellently for people also includes sensitivity to the significant needs of people in the broader community. People who have no church still get married and have funerals. The church should be known as a place where unchurched people can be served or at least directed to services the congregation cannot provide.

The desperate fiancé down the street. Consider an example of mediocre caring. A church has a policy that the minister will perform marriage ceremonies only for congregants and other believers who have counseled with the pastor for several weeks. A frantic young woman from the neighborhood calls the pastor. She and her fiancé have just learned that he will be shipped overseas in a week. They have been planning to wed, but now desire a ceremony in the next few days. The pastor denies her request because she isn't a member of the church and won't be able to complete the classes on time. Should the pastor suggest a local minister who will perform the service? Should he bend his church's rules, given the unusual nature of the request? What would be a more excellent way of caring?

Caring for Real Persons over Cold Principles

What church leaders might miss in such cases is that people are more important than policies. The pastor has a great opportunity to connect with a woman who will be a stateside military wife and who just might be interested in a church that will remain alongside her while her husband is overseas. The example illustrates a conflict between church policies and the needs of real people coming unexpectedly to the church for care. The legalistic pastor and others in leadership need to get past the otherwise fitting church rules to consider the woman's particular circumstances. The leadership could defend the rules, saying there must be consistency, good order, and integrity in the church's decisions. Of course! But people's lives are not always so consistent and well-ordered. Outsiders often don't understand such seemingly uncaring church culture. The more we force them during such unusual situations to fit the formal mold of church culture, the less we will see them let alone serve them.

In his Sermon on the Mount, Jesus says that God's laws must not be ignored. But he also says that we must search our hearts and administer love according to the needs of the person before us. He declares in Matthew 5:19 that greatness in the Kingdom is linked to obedience to the spirit and the message of the Old Testament (the Law and the Prophets). He follows this statement with the sixth commandment—don't murder. But he interprets and applies that commandment by considering people's hateful feelings and attitudes, not just their literally murderous actions. Jesus contrasts hateful attitudes with the heartfelt attitudes of love and forgiveness.

To Jesus, obedience is extremely important, but it should flow from the inner self (the heart) to external actions. When people begin with the right heart, their actions will build positive, life-affirming relationships, such as going to the sister or brother with whom one has a problem and being reconciled (Matt. 18). Jesus doesn't teach old legalisms (an eye for an eye) or new legalisms. Instead, he urges followers to gain personal integrity by unifying their hearts and their actions in the vertical love of God and the horizontal love others. Jesus teaches the true path of obedience—forming a loving heart that prompts the right actions.

The Medieval church frequently held that the common people could not and should not read or even possess a Bible—certainly not one in their own language. This was a firm, well-established church policy. Because of it, many suffered and even died. When Martin Luther challenged the policy he was supposedly asked, "What if every pot boy and swine herder had the Bible in his own language?" Luther allegedly replied, "Then we might have more Christians!" Ezekiel 34 condemns the leaders of the Old Testament church for abandoning the people. God told them that if they wouldn't shepherd his people, he would do it in their place. We risk biblical injunction if we quickly turn away people because they don't immediately fit our church policies. Policies are extremely important, but when it comes to caring compassionately and excellently for people, we shouldn't use such policies as ends in themselves.

Setting Cultural Boundaries

Heartfelt caring never means wholesale violation of clear biblical norms. What if a neighborhood group wants to use the sanctuary for a no-holds-barred bachelor party? The church doesn't have to rent its sanctuary to this group simply because the congregation is committed to caring about people. A vision of care doesn't mean that anything goes and anybody and everybody gets whatever they happen to desire. Rather, the issue is that we as a church may need to suspend our cultural traditions and policies because caring for actual persons is more important than legalistically following our own cultural rules. Often the hard, discerning work of the church is making tough calls and taking reasonable risks, not inflexibly maintaining the status quo at all costs.

What kind of message is your church sending to people who enter your doors? What are the direct and the subtle messages? What attitude is delivered from the pulpit, via the door greeter, or through the person sharing the bathroom with the visitor? It won't take long for the inquiring person to sense whether your church cares for them. The visitor will quickly see whether or not your congregation is an inflexible, insider group that has constructed walls of rules and traditions—and whether an outsider will have difficulty penetrating the hard, cold shell.

The working vision of caring for people means risk, struggle, and mistakes. The reward is knowing that the heart of Christ's church is broken for the benefit of people both within and beyond the church walls. What a joy to know that in your church the sheep and potential sheep have not been abandoned by the shepherds, and the lost have not been thrown into the cold. Proverbs 14 says that a clean stall has no ox, but it thereby lacks a harvest. If there is an ox in the stall, the stall will get messy, but there will be a harvest. Significant ministry is messy, but messy ministry is necessary for a harvest. No mess, no caring ministry beyond the barn's gate. No Kingdom vision.

Discussion Questions

1. Do congregants complain that there's too much emphasis in some churches on love and not enough on doctrinal truth? Do you know of any such congregations? How do you know that they are really that way?

2. How does your congregation care for needy people such as the sick and elderly? Does it seem to care equally for repeat visitors? For non-members who attend regularly? Explain why or why not.

3. Is the preaching and teaching in your church both biblically doctrinal and relevant? Should it be more of one or the other? Why?

4. Are you comfortable with the idea of letting your church leaders go beyond what is traditionally acceptable in church life to care for people in unique situations—maybe even to "bend" the rules/policies? If so, when? If not, please explain the kind of situation(s) or rules that would most concern you.

7

Capturing Your Biblical Working Vision

As I mentioned earlier, when my congregation established an in-house ministry for returning citizens (ex-offenders), some people began raising legitimate concerns. If there were going to be returning citizens in the church building at the same time children or young people were meeting, were the young ones safe? We considered the matter carefully, realizing that our working vision of caring for people must address the needs of the children and the parents as well as the returning citizens. We didn't want to deny building access to those who had been in prison. But we also didn't want to see our families put at risk or even leave the church.

As we emphasized the overall vision of caring for people, the congregation came to accept the new ministry and worked together to find solutions. The goal of serving returning citizens became part of our mission. It took careful regulation of scheduling (no children's groups and returning citizen groups were to be in the building concurrently). It required careful monitoring of the children (an entire section of the building was remodeled to seal off the children's area). It required education of both the families (to watch their kids) and the returning citizens (to respect the congregation's wishes and stay out of some sections of the building). The result was that no family left the church and many returning citizens are being successfully mainstreamed into the congregation. It took time, work, and planning based on our calling to serve returning citizens. Ironically, we created new rules in order to protect our ministry to real people, but the rules demonstrated our caring for everyone concerned.

A church may talk about its love for people, but is the congregation passionately focused *on caring for actual people*—not just on the concept of people "in general"? If so, which people are to be served—rich, poor, contemporary, traditional, mainstream, mavericks, ethnic majorities and minorities, and more? Are the church's commitment and passion such that the congregation is willing—as led by the Spirit—to clarify and even amend rituals, traditions, and rules to take on the messy tasks of caring for specific, broken people?

One way to analyze your own congregation's openness to serving people is to consider its attitude toward change. What is your congregation willing to change itself—and what would it never alter? Where would it be on the continuum illustrated below?

On the left of this continuum of change would be a church with a tightly closed attitude toward change. Such a rigid congregation is most concerned with doing everything properly and preserving itself. Change is frightening because it might lead congregants to do something improperly or to lose something that it holds close to its heart. This kind of "proper-and-preserving" attitude leads to keeping the church the way it is—on maintaining the status quo. It means preserving existing worship styles and maintaining the same look of the sanctuary and the identical color of the people in the pew. Many such congregations understandably don't want to lose their traditions and become too worldly. In fact, there is much about what it means to be a Christian congregation that shouldn't be given up. But when all change is threatening to a church it simply can't grow numerically or spiritually. It becomes a sleepy maintenance ministry.

On the right side of the spectrum would be a church with a wide-open attitude toward change. For such congregations—although there are not many—change is what church is all about. These congregations follow the latest fads and fashions in everything from worship style to evangelism programs. The church becomes a revolving door of hit-and-miss innovations. Some churches hold this wide-open attitude toward change because they genuinely want to reach out to lost souls. Many such congregations truly desire to serve people—even to serve everyone. This type of church vigorously values propagation and people. But it's not always clear to such a congregation what it is that makes the church distinctly Christian.

So where is your church on the continuum? I would suggest that dynamic churches are always closer to the propagation-and-people side than to the proper-and-preserving side. Although both ends of the continuum have their own difficulties, a congregation that can't imagine itself somewhere closer to the propagation-and-people side is simply not spiritually healthy. It has lost its vision for growth—and for serving people beyond its walls. It might even have lost some of its faith in what God could do through its willingness to reach out to people as well as up to God. There will always be some objections to *any* emphasis on propagation and people. But what are such objections? How do they relate to the overall concern a church may have with a working vision that's focused on caring for people? How do such concerns relate to a mission statement based on serving particular people who might not be culturally identical to existing church numbers?

Considering the Objections

OBJECTION ONE
If we emphasize serving particular people, especially outsiders, what will happen to our primary goal of faithfully glorifying God?

If serving people means compromising glory to God, then we must deny people and first serve God. If our attempt to serve any person means we seriously violate what is sacred to God and what fulfills his will for us, then we must deny the suggested service of others. If, however, caring for particular persons or groups means we're violating a congregational rule, we first need to ask if the rule is uniquely from God or from the church's inscripturated culture. Are we limited by a rule or policy that has become an end in itself? If so, are we unfaithful because we lack courage in messy ministry situations?

51

OBJECTION TWO

Since we can't please everybody, aren't we just going to create confusion so no one is truly being served?

If you bend a rule for one person, will others necessarily be hurt or offended? Will you set bad precedents? Such concerns are understandable. These are tough problems. On the other hand, the apostle Paul tells us that the law can kill but the Spirit gives life (2 Cor. 3:6). Yes, the church risks being inconsistent wherever it lives beyond the letters of its laws. But the risk on the side of caution and rigidity is that a church coldly ignores the unique and often unpredictable ministry opportunities of the very people it's called to serve.

Decisions addressing the variety of people's needs can be at the discretion of the pastor and other church leaders. Generally the decisions will necessarily be very private. The important thing is that the pastor and church leaders agree ahead of time to be flexible and compassionate rather than rigid and uncaring. They agree to trust each other's decisions regarding people even as they seek each other's advice in particularly perplexing situations. The church leaders also must teach the congregation that there may be some apparent inconsistencies in the handling of particular people and situations. The congregants must be taught that caring for people is the church's working vision. Congregants must learn that there will be situations they don't understand, but they should trust the leaders to make caring decisions. Some decisions may seem wrong or senseless, but someone's ox is stranded and needs to be rescued (Prov. 14), and there will be messiness as well as a harvest.

OBJECTION THREE

Are we going to change the church just to please a few?

Changing the church just to please a few people is not a legitimate working vision for a church. It's not right or fair to abruptly change the fabric of the congregation just to satisfy a handful of people unless it's a new church. Many congregants have been in the church for years and have sacrificed greatly to form and develop the congregation. They have been loyal in the good and bad times. They have given considerable time and money. They ministered faithfully.

But times, needs, and ministries invariably change. While it isn't fair to abruptly wrench valuable traditions away from the faithful, it isn't proper for the faithful to ignore emerging needs and opportunities for ministering to real people. Solving the tension between loyalty to the past and change for the future demands wisdom (James 1). Normally change should be slow, deliberate, and loving. Gordon MacDonald's *Who Stole My Church* rightly stresses the need for time, patience, discussion, understanding, and congregational involvement in shaping the future. The congregation's mission is not the purview of merely its leaders.

As the church reshapes itself for the future, however, it must continue to demand excellence. Sometime a church thinks it's being contemporary, for example, simply because worship includes a guitar and drums. But mediocre musicians can lead to dismal worship in traditional or contemporary worship. Excellence and compassion together encourage those coming through the door to stay. Excellence even in new ministries encourages long-time members to support new ventures.

Gradually, with compassion, conversation, understanding, and healthy pride, a congregation becomes willing to change for the good. While change is happening, the leaders must remember to regularly teach from Scripture the working vision (caring for people) and to mention the congregation's own mission statement (*who* the congregation is and *to whom* and *how* it is called to minister). The change isn't for change's sake, but for people's sake and to the glory of God. Every change must relate to the general working vision and support the specific mission statement. So must existing ministries.

Holding the working vision in front of the congregation will keep leaders sensitive to the needs of faithful traditionalists while connecting with new people. Every corner of the church must be asking two questions: (1) Is what we're doing—whether old or new—truly fulfilling the working vision of caring for people? and (2) Is what we're doing in tune with our specific mission statement?

OBJECTION FOUR

Isn't this caring stuff just another liberal do-gooder attempt to water down the Gospel and replace it with a purely "social gospel" that lacks salvation through Christ alone?

There is a huge difference between watering down the message and introducing needed change. Cultural transition by itself doesn't automatically mean the message is lost or compromised. Moreover, the "social gospel"— the idea that the church is called to provide for people's physical over their spiritual needs—is not the same as a holistic vision that seeks to save *and* help those in need. When a congregation focuses on people, it must consider their salvation, not just their emotional or physical needs. In other words, a faithful congregation cares for people's souls, not just their bodies.

Adopting a care-oriented working vision will often first appear to weaken biblical teachings. The reason is that congregations frequently define biblical Christianity by rigid traditions. Churches with rigid cultural traditions or inflexible methods of presenting biblical teachings will often appear to be deeply biblical. Therefore, any change seems to suggest that this deeply biblical church will now be shallow and more liberal, diminishing its commitment to Scripture and its proclamation of the Word. A congregation needs to guard against becoming either just a "social service" or a "gospel service." To care for the souls of living people is to care for them as whole people. This is why the work of mercy is so critical for every congregation. Caring for people and proclaiming the Gospel go hand-in-hand. Otherwise a church suffers from what Carl F. H. Henry in 1947 called *The Uneasy Conscience of Modern Fundamentalism.* "A Christianity without a passion to turn the world upside down is not reflective of apostolic Christianity," wrote Henry (16).

Beyond Sabbath Rules

I experienced this concern about remaining faithfully biblical as a child growing up in a Christian community that prized Sunday Sabbath observance. The church laws for Sunday were rigid: no ball playing, bike riding, sun bathing, swimming, TV viewing, or shopping. Of course we worshiped and studied the Bible on Sundays, but to us children the day tended to be defined more by what we couldn't do than by what we could do.

By contrast, my wife and I raised our children without such inflexible rules. Our family celebrated Sunday by enjoying the day. This meant eating together and relaxing at home through the afternoon. Now that our children are adults, they continue to worship on Sunday and to enjoy the entire day. They do so without realizing that ball playing and bike riding used to be forbidden. Their spirituality and faith are healthy and strong. A more open attitude toward Sunday didn't destroy or diminish their faith. Probably the opposite is true. They seem to practice Sabbath rest more healthfully than my generation did. They are less likely during the rest of the week to think that their human effort will "save" them from faithlessness.

Changing church practices doesn't necessarily mean weakening the biblical message. There could even be a stronger, more biblical faith if solid teaching in the home and church is combined with attractive role models and significant care for people.

Considering Impressive but Ineffective Preaching

Similarly, consider the "proper" style versus the real impact of preaching. In my church tradition, sermons were often delivered with sophisticated language, heavy doctrinal terminology, and lecture-like dispassion. For some people, such sermons and their delivery were often viewed as profound.

But there are many ways to present the same message, using different words, images, and delivery styles. A professional-sounding sermon won't necessarily connect with listeners. The same doctrine could be addressed in a more personally meaningful and relevant way.

I remember a Christian newspaper that once editorialized about two preachers in the same town. Using a pizza analogy, the editor characterized one preacher's style as a slice of thick but cold pizza. The editor described the other preacher's style as a hot but thin slice of pizza. After reading the article I decided to study the two sermons. Both sermons were biblical and doctrinal. Neither one was actually deeper than the other one, but the "thin" communicator seemed more shallow apparently because his style was more accessible. If the sermon themes were identical, which congregation was probably learning and growing more? Impressive sermon transmission is not the same as effective sermonic communication.

Finally, perhaps a reluctance to focus on caring for people is a sign of lost or diminished passion for serving Christ. Matthew 25 is clear that caring for people has eternal implications. Jesus warns the churches in Asia Minor (Rev. 2, 3) of the danger of losing their first love. Could love of tradition hide a lack of passion for serving Christ? There were churches described in Revelation 2 and 3 that looked great on the outside, but were very weak on the inside. How terrible if a church only looks faithful because it meets traditionally low expectations! In *The Vindication of Tradition*, church historian Jaroslav Pelikan says *tradition* is the "living faith of the dead," whereas *traditionalism* is the "dead faith of the living" (65). Distinguishing between the two is one of the enduring tasks of every faithful congregation.

Discussion Questions

1. Where does your church stand on the continuum between being a proper-and-preserving or a propagation-and-people congregation? How do you know? What one or two significant church conflicts or accomplishments in your church during the last three years would indicate where your congregation really stands on the continuum?

2. Would your congregation agree that a vision of caring for people requires a church to be on the propagation-and-people side of the continuum? Explain.

3. Proverbs 14:4 says, "Where there are no oxen, the manger is empty, but from the strength of an ox comes an abundant harvest." What is the point—and how might that point relate to your congregation?

4. Discuss each of the four listed objections to a congregational working vision focused on caring for people. Do you agree more with the objections or the responses? Why?

8

Avoiding Judgmentalism

I once asked a retired person in the church to assist in worship. After the event, several members told me they didn't appreciate having this man up front during worship. They didn't like the person and informed me that they had a difficult time participating because he took part. I responded, "That's wrong!" I told the critic that the retired member is a child of God, an image-bearer of Christ. The critical members needed to get over their prejudices, see beyond their emotions, and recognize the unity of all brothers and sisters in Christ.

Human nature makes us more comfortable with people who are like us. If we have a choice, we will surround ourselves with people who look and sound just like us. This is why people who tend to dress similarly are most likely to huddle in groups before and after Sunday worship.

Unfortunately, human nature sometimes works against hospitality and inclusion in the church. In fact, the nastier side of self-selecting our congregational friends is *judgmentalism—judging as inferior those who aren't like us.* We all do it, sometimes even subconsciously. We fail to accept Scripture as the only genuine source of truth regarding how we and others should live.

A congregation with a working vision of caring for people must adopt *a culture of non-judgmentalism.* Encouraging Christians to be non-judgmental is often not popular. To some, the word "non-judgmental" suggests an anything-goes attitude. To others, non-judgmentalism means "whatever"—you do your thing and I'll do mine; neither my neighbor nor I have any business judging anyone else's "private life." My fellow believers may do whatever they wish—and it's always okay with me. After all, I don't want others telling me how to live!

This laissez-faire attitude isn't biblical non-judgmentalism. It certainly isn't the non-judgmentalism recommended for congregations seeking to care for people. To understand biblical non-judgmentalism, think of judgment as negative attitudes that lead to snooping into another person's life, sticking one's nose in where it doesn't belong, holding a person's private life up for public scrutiny. Think of gossip, slander, jealousy, and even hate. These are the attitudes and actions Jesus addresses in Matthew 7—"Judge not!" Biblical non-judgmentalism means respecting my biblical neighbor (anyone in need) as well as fellow believers. It doesn't mean agreeing on everything. It doesn't mean everyone does their own thing.

Is there a time to care more personally about my neighbor's life—even to judge? Yes! Scripture teaches us to care about a person's sin (James 5). Jesus shows us how to approach a brother or sister we believe is doing us wrong (Matt. 18). The authentically biblical church will hold congregants accountable for truly unbiblical action and won't tolerate the blatant abuse of God's clear commands (1 Cor.; 2 Thes. 3). But we have to be sure that someone's actions have been truly unbiblical, a barefaced rejection of God's clear commands. Then we have to approach such people compassionately rather than judgmentally.

A caring church must be a safe place for everyone, including those who aren't like us. When a person can come to church in all his or her uniqueness and not be scorned, gossiped about, maligned, or discriminated against, the church is a safe place to step foot into and to be one's self. Most neighborhoods are full of people who will never enter a church building. Many of these people are burned out, beaten up, discouraged, cynical, and angry. They have been picked apart, talked about, shunned, and thoroughly judged by self-righteous people even though their sin may have been nothing more than irritating Christians who found the "outsiders" a little too different for their self-righteous tastes.

Of course, those hurting people who stay away from church may be mistaken; their hurt may not have been the church's fault whatsoever. Maybe they even brought some of the pain on themselves. Perceptions are strong.

If a person perceives judgment, the feelings of judgment for them are real. Conversely, if a church can develop a reputation of tangible, ongoing care, even hurting or angry people might return to fellowship.

Three key aspects of judgmentalism for churches to address are *source*, *style*, and *patience*. In the rest of this chapter, I examine source. In the next chapter, I consider style and patience.

Identifying the Source of Judgment

The Bible is the source of truth. It reveals right and wrong. The Bible must be the only standard for determining the appropriate or inappropriate admonition of congregants. When a visitor walks through the church door, however, they don't first directly engage the Word of God as a book. They engage people. The people of the church—the pastor, greeter, usher, and fellow pew-sitter—*become* the Word to a visitor. The Gospel message is first presented implicitly in the very words and actions of the church's people.

While traveling one Sunday, I visited a Lutheran church several blocks from my hotel. The pastor welcomed visitors and announced that a woman would be walking the aisles with a basket of bread for first-time visitors. The pastor said, "If you're here for the first time just raise your hand to receive our gift." I raised my hand and was invited to choose a loaf from a basket of nicely wrapped specialty breads. I'm not recommending this practice for all churches, but I do think that those congregants sent me a biblical message that Sunday. They demonstrated that they cared about me even though they had no idea who I was or if I would ever return again.

What if I moved to that city and began attending that Lutheran church? The congregation's message to me would then move beyond bread baskets and verbal welcomes. The content of congregation's actions—the pastor's word choice, the traditions of the people, and so on—would all send me a clear message about whether I had a chance of fitting into this body of Christ. Initially, however, the gift of bread by itself ensured that my wife and I would have considered re-visiting that congregation. That church's "statement" to me was nothing short of the love of Jesus for a stranger.

Saying "I Care" Without Using Words

If the words of the congregational leaders and the actions of the people suggest cultural narrowness rather than soundly biblical ideas and attitudes, a visitor will pick up on something other than God's Word and might quickly feel judged. As I mentioned, the immediate *source* of the church's message to a visitor isn't the Bible per se, but the expressed opinions, words, actions, and lifestyles of the leaders and members. In other words, a congregation's non-biblical culture can become an implicit form of judgmentalism rooted in a faulty *source*, namely, cultural preferences.

Clearly all groups have traditions and rituals. This is natural, normal and expected. Even good! But what a church does with its cultural practices is critical. Unfriendly cultural practices give a self-righteous flavor and personality to a church. If cultural practices become the source of the message, however, the congregation has replaced Scripture with its own self-righteous attitudes and actions. What does your congregation implicitly "say" to visitors? Do they truly feel welcome? Do they feel "different" and "judged"?

A church should never apologize for its unique people. But the message source must always be biblically deliberate. The church's actions should say, "Come and enjoy us and let us enjoy you. Come and let us discover and share the truth together as best we can. You may have to adjust a bit to understand us and we're willing to adjust a bit to understand you. It will be a mutual adventure! But by grace we'll become one in Christ."

When visitors or new members feel respected for who they are, the church is safe. The congregation's culture becomes a place to be without fear of rejection or embarrassment. The safe place is also a healing place of growth, and a place of becoming all that God has created a person to be. Never underestimate what God can accomplish even through the most seemingly unimpressive or wildly unique visitor.

Practicing Truth and Hospitality

Out of fear or a legitimate concern for the church, a devout member may say, "So, we should cheapen the Word of God and stop being a true church just to make outsiders comfortable?" No. But the church should work hard at forming a community which lives out actual biblical truth rather than mere cultural preferences. In fact, a church that clearly presents and proclaims biblical truth and godly expectations will risk being unpopular to some outsiders. The church must be certain that it's a source of truth and its teaching of biblical standards is truly God's Word. This must be true even on such potentially controversial topics as drunkenness, adultery, stealing, bitterness, hate, gossip, addiction, laziness, the occult, unbelief and more. When a congregation affirms its commitment to service, purity, compassion, worship, love, giving, and the like, it must be careful not to assume that such worthy goals and practices can always be easily related to culture.

A church that carefully teaches biblical attitudes and actions—especially the love of Jesus Christ—will discover that new persons will listen and respect what is taught and lived in the congregation. God puts his testimony in each person he calls to discipleship, so that the Bible speaks through them and so that they will listen. Also, if a person rejects the biblical message and leaves such a church, the cause then isn't the words, attitudes, and actions of the leaders and members. If the departing person subsequently complains, it's because of the hardness of their own heart, not the church's judgmentally inhospitable culture.

Discussion Questions

1. Is the difference between biblical and unbiblical ideas of non-judgmentalism accurate or helpful for your church? Why or why not?
2. How might your congregation have been judgmental when it should not have been? Were the situations related to cultural or biblical differences among people? To Sabbath observance?
3. Was it a good idea for the Lutheran church to give visitors loaves of bread? How about the fact that some visitors might wish to remain anonymous?
4. What is the concept of "source" when it comes to judgmentalism in congregations? Does it help you understand judgmentalism and its effects on churches? Explain.

9

Being Patient with Style

When you walk the halls of a college or the corridors of a shopping mall, you discover that most people aren't naturally inclined to establish eye contact and be cordial. In such public settings, most people remain aloof and disinterested in others, partly because they don't want to cause embarrassment. But church members carry these patterns into church. They look past unfamiliar faces in search of smiling friends. They don't always see strangers as brothers and sisters in Christ—as family members. I've often witnessed church members standing in a cluster of friends while a visitor stands just feet away, alone. In most cases the problem isn't that regular attendees are opposed to caring for others. They just don't think about or know how to practice acceptance. When they do reach out, however, they help communicate that the church is a warm and inviting place—a safe community. When a church is a safe place, evangelism happens seamlessly as part of congregational life (Acts 2).

This chapter examines how judgmentalism is communicated through a church's interactive *style*, especially through its *impatience*. I suggest that *style* (how people consciously and subconsciously act, including how they communicate) shapes how people perceive messages. Style can unwittingly communicate judgment of others. Church members are called to communicate God's love partly by example—by character, especially by the fruit of the

Spirit. People who do so are invaluable members of Christ's body of believers. Their style especially demonstrates patience with themselves, others, and God.

Doing Church in Style

The idea of style is linked to the power of acceptance and rejection. I examined in chapter eight the message source—*what* a church communicates to new persons. I now examine *how* a congregation communicates through style.

For example, the pastor's speaking and preaching style sends a message of acceptance or rejection. I remember a visiting speaker at the seminary I attended. The presenter wisely warned us aspiring ministers to be careful. He said there would be people in the congregation on Sunday who would want to talk with someone. Would they choose the pastor? The decision about whether or not to speak with us, he said, would not always be based on exactly *what* we said from the pulpit, but often on *how* the person felt about us personally as we preached. "What nonverbal messages will you send?" the speaker asked us. Years ago a member of my church remarked, "On my first visit to the church I watched your facial expression and decided this should be my church." I'm not sure exactly what the person meant, but the idea was clear. I must have acted warmly and conveyed acceptance rather than judgment.

So, what's my point? Should a pastor always dress in jeans and constantly smile? Maybe, but probably not. In any case, a church leader must always have that sense of being "on stage." The pastor and other church leaders need to say to themselves over and over again: "People are watching me and deciding if they can trust me, if they can believe me and allow me to be their pastor." Style is not quite that easy to master in the church. But church leaders need to recognize that their entire lives "speak" for the congregation. They are called to imitate Christ. Even more, they are called to "be" Christ to those they serve.

Trusting in Style

People followed Jesus because he spoke with authority. Therefore, leaders must always be ready to teach and counsel partly by modeling the love of Jesus Christ. The way leaders conduct themselves influences how people interpret and receive the messages from the pulpit, in the classroom, at the counseling chair, amidst the narthex entryway, and the like. Truthtelling from biblical sources is essential. But congregations also evaluate speakers' authenticity on the basis of eye contact, delivery, gestures, voice, and other nonverbal communication.

A huge part of successful communication is trust. The leader must think about genuineness, consistency, honesty, warmth, and joy. For instance, a sermon doesn't begin and end in the pulpit, just like a Sunday school lesson doesn't begin and end in the classroom. The extent to which a message will be understood and embraced may well start with a handshake at the door, a phone call, a visit, a casual conversation in the lobby, or a short chat at a church picnic. A Christian leader must avoid displays of irritation and defensiveness when challenged or questioned. A leader must learn to listen with ears, eyes, and posture. The ways identifiable leaders carry themselves "speak" just as much as their words. Church leaders at all levels need to convey this message to others: "You are truly important to me." If a leader has this kind of caring, compassionate *style*, an attendee is more likely to think to themselves, "Maybe I could dare to trust in the God of these people because I feel accepted and appreciated by them and their leaders."

In fact, this authentic, loving style shaped Christ's own ministry to those in need. Jesus could get plenty angry with arrogant, self-righteous people. But with humble, honest people of even little or no faith he was loving in substance and style. A church visitor thinks, "If this leader cares and even acts like they care, could it be that God cares? A person once said to me, "I believe what you teach. I'm not sure I know exactly what you teach, I just know I believe it." Such emerging faith is step one. The person didn't yet understand the Bible's message, but was getting ready to accept it as she came to understand it, partly through the style of delivery.

Modeling Loving Styles of Congregational Communication

The communicative styles of other congregants is equally important. The members are also sending messages just by attending. They're part of the "content" of the church's faithful message just by *being* what the Bible teaches. *How* they carry themselves communicates acceptance or rejection. The common congregant often doesn't know this intuitively. They need to be taught how their style communicates. The best teaching includes role modeling that matches the lessons.

The essential patterns of nonjudgmental, trusting, compassionate style that should be taught to the congregation may include the following ten personal commitments and practices:

1. I consciously look for new faces, smile, and simply say, "Hi."
2. I attempt to welcome and to sit next to people I don't know rather than always in the same place or with the same people.
3. I don't leave church right away. I stay to talk and listen, moving from person to person and group to group.
4. I seek out the list of people requesting prayer and not only pray for them, but regularly send cards or notes to the people listed in the bulletin, mentioned in prayers, or announced at worship.
5. I refuse to talk about anybody—their private business, their uniqueness, their dress, and their actions—except positively and affirmingly.
6. I refuse to condemn, criticize, or mock any congregant in the room or elsewhere.
7. I learn the working vision—caring for people—and the related statement of mission, and I verbalize them to others and verbally support programs and ministries that truly care for people.
8. I don't resist change if I see that it truly benefits people and helps the church fulfill its mission.
9. I personally welcome and congratulate anyone who is welcomed to the church or baptized during a Sunday service.
10. I let others in the church see me talking and laughing with a person who may not look like most other attendees.

There are many more things to learn and do than these ten, but they are good start toward becoming a stylistically self-aware congregation. A church's style can create a culture of love, acceptance, and safety. People won't automatically gravitate toward the unknown; they won't naturally create a culture of acceptance. By nature, people tend to lapse into their old ways of privacy and aloofness. A naturally learned "closedness" could say to a stranger or new member, "We don't trust you. Your presence disturbs us. We're better off if you're not here." Learning an open, nonjudgmental style will create a new atmosphere that says, "Welcome—and we really do mean it." Leaders need to model such style so that the entire congregation desires to do likewise.

Being Patient

Moving as a congregation toward modeling nonjudgmental caring for people doesn't come easily. There are no quick techniques for creating a nonjudgmental style. It takes a long-term commitment to reviving a church's culture, from its unspoken attitudes to its unexamined actions. It can't happen successfully just from the pulpit or simply through formal classes; the whole congregation has to join in by modeling care. Leaders and members passionate for a church that is a safe place realize it may take many months or even a few years to become an openly caring congregation.

The training must not be rushed. Members must not feel that a new (or newly inspired) pastor, council, session, or board is going to change them overnight. In fact, overzealous church leaders may themselves come off as judgmental—exactly what they're teaching people to avoid. Members also need time to get used to the very idea of change. Any heavy-handed, forced change will meet considerable resistance. Too often people experience this kind of disrespectfully mandated change at their workplaces, and they're leery of the same attitudes and actions settling into their church's leadership team. Real, heartfelt change requires patience.

Demonstrating Patience

Teaching patience begins not just in pulpits and the classrooms, but also in hallways and homes. The training is spoken but also modeled. The training is gentle, friendly, careful, and divided into small chunks the congregation can digest. Leaders must first win the confidence of the congregation by proving that they themselves are safe before convincing the congregation to be a safe people. Teaching patience requires being patient.

A congregation should be patient with itself, too. After all of the leader training, members eager for change will still observe other members telling a racial joke (right after the sermon on love), criticizing "that lady's weird hairdo," complaining that the church spends too much on evangelism, and discrediting elements of that morning's worship service. Crudeness, unkindness, and negative attitudes will occur along the way. Some people will continue to feel threatened by any congregational changes.

The congregation needs time to absorb a working vision of what it genuinely means to care for people. Congregants need time to see, understand, and embrace such a vision for themselves. It takes time and patience for a people-focused culture to form. Even when it does, there will still be mistakes, awkward moments, and stupid blunders—by everyone, including the official leaders. No one will be able to walk the talk immediately or perfectly. The leaders in this process thereby include everyone in the congregation who begins the process of being a caring congregation by modeling it for others. Such leaders need to live the working vision and always be patient with congregants who are learning how to do so.

Sometimes the members who do understand the working vision of caring for people can become irritated and impatient with those members who don't seem to care or are even opposed to it—even if they never express their concerns during church meetings and at learning opportunities. Enthusiastic members who have joined the campaign against uncaring judgmentalism can themselves become judgmental of their brothers and sisters in Christ. Such impatient souls might say uncharitable things about others: "They're not spiritual enough!" "They call themselves Christians?" Here again, everyone needs patience. Criticism of uncooperative members will actually impede progress. Instead, let the combined efforts of leaders and members who teach and model be the food to nurture the rest of the congregation. Patience is indeed one essential part of the fruit of the Spirit!

Visiting Patience

Finally, the congregation needs to be patient with visitors. True, there is the adventure of witnessing the arrival of new and diverse people. But the actions and appearances of visitors may well be hard for some congregants to accept.

"There's alcohol on his breath."

"She stands outside and smokes."

"They're living together without marriage."

"That young couple slouches down, arm-in-arm throughout the sermon."

"He smells."

"He talks openly about the R-rated movie with sex-scenes he saw last Sunday."

"I heard her utter a 'damn' and 'hell' while conversing today."

"She told our group she is sick of her husband and wants to 'divorce the bum.'"

"I was in their house. It's really a mess."

"I heard him brag about how much he paid for his new luxury car."

Since humans aren't naturally inclined to live out a style of acceptance and warmth, so also church members are naturally inclined to criticize, be suspicious of, and reject those who are different and who they don't personally know, let alone understand. There will often be a natural reluctance to want such different people in the church. When members are encouraged to seek and accept such people, the response may be, "What's the church coming to?" Again, the words of Martin Luther: "Maybe more Christians!"

Waiting on the Spirit

Even as we work hard, we must wait patiently for the Spirit to do its work. If I personally demand that a unique person must change or even change immediately, I may not be yielding to the Spirit's timing (the Greek *kairos*). I might not be giving the congregation time to model and mentor. If new people have attitudes or actions that offend others, let the loving atmosphere of the church and the power of the Spirit and the Word do the changing. This will take time. The Spirit's kairos.

The congregation needs to see sinners among and within its ranks. The congregation will grow by watching the joys, sorrows, successes, and failures in the spiritual growth of seekers and new and renewed believers. The congregation needs time to realize that the church is the womb and the arms of a nurturing, spiritual mother, not a cold, machine-like organization. Before, during, and after a change in life, the broken, beaten, and inexperienced people need a place of protection, forgiveness, and hope. They need spiritual mothers and fathers in the church family who are committed to nurturing them with all of the caring patience evident in the most loving and affirming families.

Partly as parental figures in the church family, leaders must prepare the congregation for this kind of congregational healing process. Leaders must teach the congregation about the presence and power of the Holy Spirit to change hearts, so that attendees can embrace the Spirit's work in their lives. The congregation needs to realize that healing and change won't be the same for everyone walking through the door. Also, the final determination regarding the extent of the church's patience with particular members must be rooted in the Spirit and not in the extent to which those persons fit the older, perhaps less-caring church culture.

Accepting Temporary Failures

Moreover, the congregation must be encouraged to accept some failures without relinquishing all hope and without rejecting slow-to-change members. Not every person who moves among the congregation will be healed and transformed; some will not stay long-term with the church. In learning patience, then, the congregation comes to realize itself as dynamic, not static; growing, not frozen. The dynamic flow is the action of accepting, modeling, and risking renewal—of lamenting lost ventures yet anticipating the arrival of persons for whom the congregation can begin caring anew.

A caring congregation comes to realize it needs to patiently anticipate God's grace in the lives of newcomers and long-term members alike. New people will bring positive, unexpected gifts to the congregation. An ex-convict, a person of color, an individual from a seemingly "foreign" culture, or someone with a unique lifestyle can help the congregation to see itself and its closedness more honestly. A visitor may bring a fresh idea or emphasis. If the congregation patiently expects God to work through outsiders, great and beautiful things will happen to the congregation as well. Then a church isn't only a safe place. A church is becoming a new place. The safe and renewed church becomes the welcoming environment spoken of in Acts 2: "And the Lord added to their number daily those who were being saved."

Discussion Questions

1. What exactly is cultural *style*? How does it relate to *source*—as discussed in the last chapter?
2. When churches become enthusiastic about their style are they simply caving in to modern marketing habits? Can styles be countercultural?
3. How would your congregation respond to the ten communicative practices described in the chapter that the author uses to guide members? Would some of them seem new? Challenging? Controversial? Guilt-inducing?
4. What would it mean for your church to be patient regarding style?

10

Becoming Humbly Spiritual

I'm examining in this book the ways the church can determine how well it's embracing and achieving a biblical working vision of caring for people. I discussed earlier the first criterion the church can use in self-evaluation, namely, its judgmentalism. I also considered the importance of modeling patient acceptance of others. In this chapter I consider how the congregation can evaluate and project its genuine *spirituality*.

The idea of Christian spirituality can be both confusing and intimidating. It can also be divisive when some congregants claim to be more spiritual or Spirit-filled than others. Christian spirituality's many definitions and elements have included:

- a mature, moderate, wise Christian lifestyle
- energetic worship with clapping and dancing
- very high moral standards in a carefully-lived, highly-disciplined life
- the use of Bible-rich language with frequent offers to others of love and prayer support
- deep theological and biblical knowledge and insights
- a simple life dedicated to Jesus and lived physically and culturally apart from the world

- being actively focused on Jesus, the center of all things
- attending discerningly to what God has done, is doing, and has promised to do

Spirituality could be one or more of all the above—as well as numerous other beliefs and practices. But a church's immediate concerns about spirituality should not be the congregation's precise definition of *true* spirituality. Rather, a church ought to consider the impact that various forms and expressions of spirituality have on its working vision and mission statement. Are your congregation's current spiritual practices and assumptions enhancing or diluting your calling to care for particular kinds of people with excellence and compassion?

Problems arise when certain congregants believe they are the supreme models of one or another kind of spirituality or they have uniquely captured what it means to be spiritual. In nearly every congregation, some members will think that their lives are the benchmark, the guideline, the ultimate expression of true spirituality. In their view, everyone else should similarly experience the life of faith. These are the *hyper-spiritual* members of any congregation.

Hyper-spiritual members are usually well meaning. We ought to appreciate their personal spiritual discoveries and godly joy. We ought to be thankful for the good they do. Such people often become a congregation's teachers, evangelists, and prayer leaders. But they can also cause significant conflicts and even drive away newcomers.

Considering Hyper-Spiritual People

Paradoxically, hyper-spiritual congregants can become a barrier to working with new or spiritually inexperienced congregants. They might impose their brand of personal spirituality on others. Hyper-spiritual members often get hooked on a new parachurch movement, Bible-study program, or means of sharing Christ with others. They have just read the latest profound book, attended an exciting seminar, or joined a new outreach movement in the community. Now they expect everyone else to wake up and similarly demonstrate their own true love for God and his Kingdom. They announce their new-found spiritual experience and expect church leaders and other members to scramble to fulfill their expectations. They're determined to get the congregation to rise to their spiritual level so that the church will become what every church supposedly needs to become spiritually.

Maybe we should accept all of the enthusiasm exuded by hyper-spiritual brothers and sisters in Christ. A church needs such hard and enthused workers. Maybe the core of the congregation does need to wake up spiritually.

But there is a line that such spiritual people can cross—the line between truly wonderful and godly faith on one side, and being determined to have everyone else become just like them on the other side. Too often such enthusiastic members expect everyone else to affirm and share their views of Christian faithfulness—their knowledge, language, experiences, physical movements in worship, and so much more. Spiritually enthusiastic members have to be careful or they can create the impression that no one else has arrived at their elevated level of spirituality.

Such holier-than-thou attitudes invariably become divisive. That's the first problem—more divisions in the congregation. Self-righteous attitudes and actions invariably divide congregations.

But there is also the potential of pushing away innocent, searching attendees. The defenseless victim of the hyper-spiritual person's effrontery is often the recent attendee, the new believer, the inexperienced church attendee, or the person with problems needing healing in the church. In my experience, the losers in this scenario are those who often need if not crave attention, and therefore are looking for someone who cares about them. Such needy and often excited people become the waiting targets for those who think of themselves as the most spiritual congregants.

At first, the needy person is enamored by the attention that hyper-spiritual people heap on them. But then two things potentially happen. First, the hyper-spiritual people inform the newcomers that the church leadership and the church as a whole aren't the most spiritually alive people. This sows doubt and divisiveness. Second, newcomers grow weary of the pressure from hyper-spiritual people. They decide to stay away from the entire church.

Both dynamics—sowing doubt and pushing for spiritual conformity—scare away new, inexperienced, needy, and even troubled people. Newcomers begin to see the church as a place that plays spiritual politics and lacks love.

If these hurting people don't give up on church altogether, they may simply believe the charge that the leadership and the congregation aren't truly spiritual and proceed to seek spiritual food elsewhere.

Addressing Hyper-Spirituality

There are at least six solutions to this problem of misusing and abusing spirituality:

1. Leaders should present opportunities for hyper-spiritual persons to express themselves by finding avenues through which such persons can exercise their excitement. Boundaries are set, but none of the spiritual folks can say, "The church doesn't care about me and my special faith experience."

2. The church should aggressively pursue a care-oriented working vision so that new, troubled, weak, and inexperienced persons will always sense and feel that the common, less hyper-spiritual people of the church truly care about them. This will diffuse any comments they pick up that their new congregation isn't adequately spiritual.

3. Leaders should be very visible and stay connected with new and needy congregants. Then, when the new and needy reach out, they will know and feel that the leadership is accessible and truly cares. Again, this diffuses the potential criticisms of hyper-spiritual members.

4. Leaders should remain ready and willing to confront any members who cross the line with their spiritual enthusiasm. If the church determines that the hyper-spiritual congregants are being divisive and scaring off people, the leaders must tell them that any efforts to promote spirituality in the congregation must be positive, supportive, and constructive. As needed, leaders can tell the hyper-spiritual members that their actions have been divisive, even unbiblical. The confrontation should warn members that divisiveness won't be tolerated because it denies all believers' union with Christ.

5. Pastors should sometimes preach sermons that explore spirituality, unity, diversity, and how to truly address the spiritual needs of people. Pastors should teach the congregation about the church as community, including how to address people and the importance of working together to achieve the biblical vision of caring for people.

6. Pastors should preach occasionally on the nature of genuine spirituality. The quiet saint in the congregation needs to know that they're indeed truly being spiritual by: sitting in prayer at the kitchen table each morning; faithfully sending the "I care" card to the sick and shut-in; gently offering words of encouragement to the person in the church lobby who has just experienced significant loss. The congregation must know that spirituality isn't only the new, loud, emotional, or exciting experience. Sermons should encourage each congregant to find their own ways that God speaks to them, and how they can grow in, and experience the joy of, their spiritual union with Christ and other believers.

Such steps can both discipline and put boundaries around hyper-spiritual persons. But they can also equip and teach other members to look positively at their own God-given spirituality. All members then see themselves as important participants in the Holy Spirit's gifts. With this affirming identity, congregants will be more willing and able to think of themselves as genuinely spiritual and to enter into the important work of caring for people. They will learn and know that a simple act like talking briefly to a new face in the lobby is an important spiritual act and can have great significance in God's Kingdom. It would not be the first time that a new believer tells the story that they were about ready to turn around and walk out of the church building on that first Sunday morning visit when, out of nowhere, a quiet, friendly person walked up to and warmly greeted them. That greeting led to the decision to stay for worship, and the worship led to the desire to return—ultimately to hear, understand and accept Jesus.

Discussion Questions for Spiritual Churchists

1. Are the bullet points at the beginning of this chapter a fitting and adequate description of spirituality? How would you revise the list?
2. How would you identify hyper-spiritual people? Are there any in your congregation? Have they generally been an asset or liability for your church? If you don't know of any, how do you think your congregation would respond to hyper-spiritual visitors? Explain.
3. Are the six solutions to misusing and abusing spiritually realistic? If not, what would you suggest for your congregation?
4. What might your church do to promote a healthy spirituality among youth and/or adults?

11

Defining Membership

A single man in his sixties living in the church neighborhood begins attending worship services. He has a classic adult conversion to Christ and joins the church. He works in several entry-level areas of ministry until he finds his niche—the evangelism calling team. After a couple of years in the church, he meets a single woman about his age. They plan marriage. Several months before the wedding, she moves into his apartment because her lease is up and they hope to wed soon.

The head of the church's calling team tells this engaged man that he must leave the team because he is practicing fornication by living with his fiancé without being married. One of the elders tells other elders that the man is already "outside" the church because of his living arrangement. The elders discuss whether the man should still be permitted to marry in the church since he was never dropped from the membership roll. A respected elder says even if the man leaves the congregation he is still a believer and therefore a member of the church of Christ. The elders are divided over the situation and wonder what to do. Meanwhile, the wedding day is rapidly approaching. How should the elders proceed?

Admitting the Complexity of Church Membership

Membership in the church is more complex than membership in most organizations. Groups such as the Kiwanis, the Masonic Lodge, and the high school basketball team know if one is or isn't a member. There's really no middle ground. In such an organization there will be clear rules, requirements, and prerequisites for membership.

At one level, the church is different. A congregation probably will have a membership list, some standards for membership, and a process to become a member. But other church-membership dynamics aren't always apparent—especially one's personal relationship with Jesus Christ.

Embracing the Mystery of Being "in Christ"

There is a mystical union, a bond of faith, an invisible relationship that makes a person a member of the one "universal" church irrespective of denominations or other categories. Everyone who trusts and lives by faith in Christ is a Christian. Everyone who follows Christ, however imperfectly, is a Christian. Sitting in the quiet of their own living room, a person could read or hear about the Gospel and then accept Christ as their Lord and savior. They could then walk down the street to the local church and enter the door as a "member" of God's church even though they are not an official member of any congregation. Even if the person gets to know congregants and applies for membership, their own faith journey will remain unique. A church may have rules and processes for membership, but each member's journey will reflect their unique experience. Why? Because the Spirit moves people to faith in endlessly diverse ways.

Congregational membership blends formal process with this mysterious, invisible dynamic that churches can't easily define and describe. In order to become a member, a believer presumably must believe in Jesus Christ—or at least claim to so believe. The Spirit blows where it will, calling people into fellowship with Jesus. We humans can't control faith. Yet each church must make judgments about who can join a congregation.

Addressing Real Cases of Church Membership

The churchless woman down the street. An elderly woman lives in the church neighborhood. The pastor visits her several times yearly at her request as part of the pastor's neighborhood ministry. She confesses faith in Christ during one of the visits. She has very little church experience and has never officially joined a congregation. She rarely worships at the church due to age and her declining health. Then she dies. Her family asks the pastor to conduct the funeral. At the funeral, the family identifies the pastor as "mom's minister" and the church as "mom's church." Was this really her church? Was she ever a member?

The widower with two homes. An elderly widower spends most of each year wintering in the South and living at a cottage in the North during the summer. He says he has been a member of his home church all his life, but now resides there less than a dozen times annually. Most congregants no longer know who he is. He faithfully mails in a tithe every month. He is a Christian, but is very quiet and private, rarely verbalizing his faith. He dies. The new pastor doesn't recognize the name when the family calls with news of the death. They refer to the church as "dad's church." Was he a member when he died?

The abused middle-age woman. A middle-age woman begins attending church. Her very hard life included abuse, poverty, prison, and drugs. The congregation and the Gospel give her new hope. She makes friends in the church and eventually commits to following Christ. She goes through the membership process and joins the church. She remains active in the church until her marriage fails and she announces she is a lesbian. She voluntarily leaves the church, lives with her lesbian friend, becomes ill, and dies. Her friends and family inform the pastor that she "never lost her faith in Christ." They ask for a Christian funeral in the church. Even though the church leaders had begun the process of excommunication, she was technically still a member. Should the pastor conduct her funeral—and in the church? Was she truly a member when she died? If not, when did she cease being a member? Why?

The unfaithful young wife considering abortion. A young couple, active in the church, calls the pastor to their home. She confesses to an affair through which she has become pregnant. They tell the pastor the affair is over and they both want pastoral counseling for the marriage. They also tell the pastor they're considering abortion since their family and friends know that the husband had a vasectomy and that they were not planning on more children. After a couple of months, they discontinue counseling and the pastor notices that she shows no sign of pregnancy. Has she had the abortion? She is a Sunday school teacher. Should the pastor challenge her right to teach? Should he notify elders and discipline the couple—even if the pastor pledges confidentiality to counselees? Does he remain silent and permit them to continue as regular members? What does their membership really mean?

The engaged but unequally yoked couple. A young couple approaches the woman's pastor to perform their marriage. She has been a member of the church since birth and has publicly professed her faith, officially joining the church. He isn't a church member and never has been—anywhere. The minister refuses to marry them because they're "unequally yoked" (2 Cor. 6). They get married elsewhere and return some years later to talk with the minister. The man reports that he has become a Christian through the love of the pastor who married them and the love of their new congregation. The woman says that when the wedding occurred she "didn't really believe a thing"; she had joined the church as a teen only to satisfy her parents. So, at the time of the wedding, were they actually both non-members? Should the pastor have married them?

The gatekeeper-minister maintaining high standards for church membership. A conservative minister speaks to a high school youth group. The minister declares that no one who has been divorced without provable adultery is permitted to join his church. One of the teenagers asks if such a person can go to heaven. "Of course," says the minister, "if they believe in Christ." "Then," replies the group, "why can't they join your church?" The minister replies, "Believing in Christ is one thing, joining the church is quite another." The teen leaves. Is the minister correct?

The church neighbors looking after one another. A young man leaves his home church when he marries a believer from a different denomination. His parents reject him. Decades go by and he never again attends or joins a church. He lives in a highly churched neighborhood, just a short walk from two major congregations. After the man's death, his next-door neighbors—strong believers and active church members—speak to the man's Christian relatives at the funeral home. The neighbors assure the relatives that "he is with the Lord. Even though he didn't go to church, he met with us often for Bible study and prayer. We were his congregation." True? Can a group of neighbors be a church? Can you belong to such a church and be considered a "church member"?

The active members refusing membership. Two adult men decide together to remove their names and their families' names from the church official membership roster. They promise to continue tithing, attending, worshiping, and serving. They just want their names off the list. Why? They joined a political movement after reading books published by the group that convinced them that if they were legal members and someone sued the church they could lose all their possessions. After their names are removed, are they still members?

These examples are based on actual situations I've encountered. Each situation presents a unique challenge regarding boundaries of church membership. What are the practical, spiritual, legal, and eternal meanings of membership? Is there a difference between going to heaven and being a member? If a person is worshiping with a congregation but not an official member, are they still in fact a member by faith and the Spirit? If so, what does that mean? Are there "church members" in the neighborhood who never attend worship services but still should be under the care of the church? Could that "church" be next-door neighbors?

The most important issue is determining what's biblical. Does Acts 2 lay down rules for formal membership? "And the Lord added daily those who were being saved" (42–47). What about Romans 9:10, which indicates that a believer is anyone who believes in her heart and publicly professes their faith in Jesus Christ?

A church committed to a working vision of caring for people may need to redefine and even expand its concept of membership. The Bible might say that church membership is: (1) simply knowing and trusting Jesus, and (2) connecting significantly with God's people, such as a profession of faith in the presence of other believers. If we make membership more than that, do we risk forms of ritualism, legalism, and traditionalism? On the other hand, if we're too informal and spontaneous, do we risk being irresponsible in Kingdom matters? In the parable of the mustard seed, Jesus says the Kingdom is large and provides a place for many (and many types?) of birds making their nests in God's flourishing Kingdom (Matt. 13:31). Just what does this mean for church membership?

Discussion Questions

1. What are the membership procedures and standards in your congregation—and why?
2. Some congregations and denominations require for membership only a simple confession of faith in Christ. Is this sufficient? Would it be sufficient for your church? Explain.
3. How would or should your church respond to each of the membership examples in this chapter—e.g., the churchless woman and the widower?
4. Read the last section of Acts 2, below. Does it appear that people became members shortly after their conversion to Christ? If so, would that work today? Would it work for your congregation? Explain.

They devoted themselves to the apostles' teaching and to the fellowship, to the breaking of bread and to prayer. Everyone was filled with awe, and many wonders and miraculous signs were done by the apostles. All the believers were together and had everything in common. Selling their possessions and goods, they gave to anyone as he had need. Every day they continued to meet together in the temple courts. They broke bread in their homes and ate together with glad and sincere hearts, praising God and enjoying the favor of all the people. And the Lord added to their number daily those who were being saved (Acts 2:42–47).

12

Setting Biblical Membership Standards

usic was the gateway to my church for a young mother in the neighborhood. She and her husband began attending. She was so drawn to the music that she quickly joined the choir. Some months later, I visited their home and discovered that she claimed to be a Buddhist. Yet through the music and personal contact with the choir members, she had become a vibrant Christian. Several years later, her husband's work forced a move to another state. They never did join my church, but their last Sunday with us was filled with hugs and tears from their fellow Christians—their fellow members.

As I indicated earlier, church membership defies clear and precise definition. Is membership legal? Spiritual? Formal? Casual? Does belonging to Christ mean automatic church membership? Should formal congregational membership require an involved process? Is someone a member who has officially joined the church but doesn't believe in their heart that Jesus died and arose?

Joining with Christ in Church Membership

It would appear that in the early church believing in Christ meant automatic and immediate membership in the church body. As I previously quoted from the book of Acts, "The Lord added to their number daily those who were being saved" (Acts 2:4–47). This membership seems to precede any formal membership in any organized group. An individual Christian and a congregation eventually must ask what this membership "with Christ" means to the congregation. What about issues of authority and responsibility in the church body? The relation of the individual to the leaders? The apparent right of the individual to enjoy all the benefits and obligations of being part of a body of Christ?

The simple answer to these membership issues might seem to be that new believers are instantly by faith a member of Christ and his universal Kingdom. In other words, *faith alone*—not any official congregational membership—seals their place in Christ's body of all believers.

Reconsidering Formal Church Membership

Nevertheless, most congregations include a more formal membership process to officially bring new believers into full, legal membership of their congregation. While such a move to process and formalize membership may be necessary and expected by both parties, at what point does it mask and somewhat dilute the dynamic character of spiritual membership "in Christ"? If joining a church is partly a mystical union with Christ and isn't akin to joining the Kiwanis or the neighborhood country club, does the church really need official membership standards?

Church leaders often insist that attending classes and promising to volunteer are reasonable and necessary expectations for full membership. Without such expectations, they suggest, maybe people won't take their membership seriously and could even drift away and disappear. New attendees just won't have the same commitment to Christ and the church if there are no membership standards. New members, some argue, won't grow in their faith. Moreover, the church won't be blessed by newcomers' presence if they aren't actively using their gifts to care for others.

As much as these cause-affect arguments for formal membership processes seem reasonable, biblical, and necessary, they fail to address two problems. First, apparently this isn't the way people joined the New Testament church. Second, the arguments may not always be true. Even well-entrenched members don't hesitate to walk away if they become bored, grow irritated, or find a church they like better. Some active members will stop attending just because they have moved more than ten miles away. Conversely, other new believers who join simply by faith, without formal membership, may participate productively for years.

Some time ago one of our prime worship leaders commented during worship when a new member was introduced, "One of these days my wife and I need to join this church; we've only been here ten years." Congregants laughed. His point was clear—they were members and everyone thought of them that way. Years later, they're still as involved as ever, and still haven't formally joined our church. They just don't like formal procedures. They prefer dynamic relations and tend to be apprehensive about formality.

Carrying New Members' Baggage

Another argument for formal membership procedures is fear about newcomers' "baggage." This is the concern that people with troubled backgrounds, damaged lives, and troubles galore should not have easy, informal membership permitting them to carry all that baggage into the church. According to this view, the membership process rightly filters out people with stained backgrounds and unresolved issues. This argument is perplexing. Isn't baggage one of the things the church cares the most about—especially the baggage of embarrassing or offensive sin?

Scripture's heroes of faith are people with considerable baggage. Jesus invites people to him who are weak and heavy laden. Bible characters loaded with baggage include Rahab, David, Peter, Paul, Matthew, Judah, and many more. None of these people took classes or seminars before being accepted by God and his people. Yet many of them may not qualify for membership in plenty of today's congregations.

Some churches really do inscripturate culture for the purpose of establishing baggage-reducing membership standards. As a result, people may join Jesus and his redeemed and redeeming community with the same kind of attitude that they might sign up for a prestigious club. For them, becoming a congregational member is like joining a social group that's jealous of its unique, ethnocentric, cultural identity.

When a new person attends a membership class or in some way submits to the scrutiny of the church, will a questionably biblical screen of culture actually guarantee that the new member has committed their life to Jesus

Christ? Would it possibly be better to make it easier for those with baggage to join so that they might grow spiritually not as aspiring members but as one of "us"?

Real Cases of Questionable Members

The distraught elder. An elderly man recalls when he was an elder in a conservative congregation during the 1950s. He had missed an elders' meeting and listened carefully as the minutes of that meeting were read the following month. The minutes told of a young woman from the congregation who came to the last elders' meeting to profess her faith and join the church. The elders refused her membership because, in attempting to answer their questions, they determined that she didn't "know enough." The elderly man tells of how he challenged the elders by asking the question, "Who of us knows enough?" The elders reconsidered, and that very evening sent two elders to her home to invite her back to church and to receive her into the church as a full member. Should a church ever refuse membership to someone who has committed their life to following Jesus Christ, even if they haven't studied most of the nuances and ramifications of the faith? How much faith is enough for membership?

The nonmember with lighter baggage. The worship leader who said he and his wife would have to join the church after ten years came from a background of heavy baggage: drugs, alcohol, divorce, imprisonment, and an immoral life on the streets. He was certainly not ready for formal membership. He was drawn by the music. He wanted to be part of the music. His life began to change. Ten years later, he had become a model of Christian service even though he still had not become an official member. Should a church refuse to treat such a person as a member even if they really don't want to join?

Saving People for Church

Perhaps the best way to deeply address the matter of membership is to begin with this question, "Is membership rooted in justification or sanctification?" *Justification* is the moment and reality of basic salvation—going from spiritual death to eternal life in Christ by faith alone (Rom. 1:16–17). At that moment of *conversion* (turning around to follow Jesus rather than living by the ways of the world), the person becomes a new creature in Christ and is adopted by God to be his child (Rom. 8). At that moment, the person is forgiven and justified, thereby becoming part of the universal church of God (Rom. 5; Acts 2).

Sanctification is the process of growing in the Lord after being justified (Rom. 12–14). Sanctification is all about becoming holier, more Christ-like. Historically, the church has approached membership as part of the sanctification process—as you grow spiritually, you grow into the church, and the church nurtures your growth. One is eligible to become a member when one has reached a specified level of biblical and doctrinal knowledge and demonstrates such knowledge by how they live. Church membership is then rooted in sanctification more than in justification. To put it differently, justification is seen as necessary but not sufficient for membership.

If membership is rooted in justification, then the primary requirement for "in-Christ" membership is faith, especially the straightforward confession of that simple faith (Rom. 10:9–10). The church would ask only for a statement of faith in Christ as the basis for membership. There would never be a long, required process of behavioral changes followed by evidence of one's sustained sanctification. The church would never suggest that it's more difficult to belong to the church than to belong to Christ.

Making justification the standard for membership may be the most biblical. Moreover, it does seem to help a church fulfill its working vision of caring for people. People aren't made to feel that they must live up to human standards of holiness to be accepted into God's family.

Using justification—or salvation—as the standard for membership can lead to this kind of concern: "You're making it too easy, so too many will join the church who aren't spiritually ready to join." This criticism could be very true, and might be the reason why churches tend to lean toward sanctification as the basis for membership. But consider what the criticism actually says: "We're making membership too easy!" I offer three responses.

Justifying Simple Membership

First, the Bible itself makes the initial bond with Christ and his people remarkably easy. Scripture normally speaks only of faith (John 3:16; Rom. 10:9–10; Acts 2:4–47; Rom. 1:16–17). Acts 2 tells us that people were added daily, with no evidence of any elaborate educational process or long-term proof of sanctification.

Second, will many new members actually abuse membership by living horribly unacceptable lives after justification? The reality is that the people of the world aren't lined up at the door of the average congregation begging to join in order to live exactly as they have been living. If a person has gone so far as to actually attend services, submit to preaching, and come to a point of professing faith, clearly they're guided by the Spirit. How else could we explain such transformation? A church should gladly welcome them rather than create the impression that the church is a tough club to join even after someone commits to following Jesus.

Third, sanctification is a lifelong process with many ups and downs amidst significant disagreements over proper conduct among Christians, denominations, and churches regarding the level required for full membership. Who ever really knows enough about Jesus? Who is sanctified beyond measure? Who is ready to join because they no longer sin? Who will cast the first stone at a sinner waiting to join? (John 8:7).

Perhaps we best serve people by making membership special, unique, and joyful, but not "clubby." Caring for people means taking risks, living on the edge, depending on the Holy Spirit. Having our processes too tidy and complete may not always be the best and most biblical way to do church membership. Would this mean we eliminate all process? Probably not. There is a place for process. The solution to membership, faith, and process may be to avoid categorizing the person and the process, and looking at the unique needs and situation of each baggage-carrying person coming through the church doors.

Discussion Questions

1. The chapter opens with the example of the Buddhist joining the church choir. Could that happen in your congregation? How would you know? Should your church be extra careful so that this sort of thing doesn't happen? If so, how would your church prevent it—and what would those procedures say about what membership means in your church?

2. At what point could new-member requirements such as membership classes and mandatory meetings prior to membership become a barrier to some enthusiastic new believers who wanted to join your church?

3. To what extend should a church be wary of people coming in with "baggage"?

4. Is justification or sanctification a better general standard for church membership? Explain each option and then discuss which would be best for your congregation.

13

Nurturing Sanctification

In his book *The Faith: What Christians Believe, Why They Believe It, and Why It Matters*, Charles Colson praises churches that require new people to sign an agreement prior to joining that commits them to congregational service and financial support (166). Personally, I applaud the spirit of this practice and its desired goal, namely, a congregation filled with people who are growing and developing in God's Kingdom through learning, living, and giving.

But must we achieve that goal by linking it to the membership process as a kind of promise of sanctification? I believe we can base membership on justification and still achieve such goals as learning, living, and giving. We don't need to confuse membership with purely human processes, no matter how noble they are. The key is to create a church atmosphere that values and practices such learning, living, and giving. In my view, a newcomer grows by doing what the Bible demands and the church expects. But such growth is part of the whole sanctification process and shouldn't be an intimidating barrier to membership.

Joining to Grow in Church

As I suggested in the last two chapters, Scripture seems to lean toward "justification by faith" as the foundation for membership. Rooting membership in justification also helps the church to realize its working vision. Justification sends the right message of faith to the new attendees and avoids the potential of expecting them to live up to church culture before they can join the highly exclusive club. We become members of Christ's church at the moment we first believe that Christ died for the forgiveness of all of our sins. No amount of "good works" is going to make us more worthy of becoming church members. The church is for redeemed sinners—the very ones for whom Jesus died and was resurrected.

Basing membership on justification doesn't mean the church should be entirely casual about new people. The church should have an ongoing array of classes, courses, and seminars for learning and growing. Membership rooted in justification doesn't eliminate or diminish "training in righteousness" (2 Tim. 3:16). Perhaps training is even more intense from this perspective since the congregation accepts new members realizing that it plays a huge role in their sanctification. The bulk of training, however, comes after rather than before membership.

The yardstick of justification does risk a person joining the church who isn't ready or doesn't really mean it. The church does take that risk. But the risk of putting human conditions on the process of membership could be worse. Church culture must never stand in the way of the believer. Jesus often opposed self-righteous religious leaders who were convinced that heaven was reserved for a select few that included them.

On the other hand, the church is also an institution that requires some attention to process. Laws exist for the church to be a valuable part of the community. Volunteers and staff must adhere to federal, state, and local laws as well as to unwritten standards of decency and good order (1 Cor. 14:40). The people of the congregation don't just come and go at will, but are tied to church schedules, policies, rituals, worship times, and places. Programs demand development, organization, and administration. There can't be a significant and caring ministry without both boundaries and clear expectations. Membership rooted in justification isn't an excuse for a congregation to be so relaxed and informal that there is sloppiness, confusion, and neglect—so that anyone can join just because they want to. Membership must not be so loosely "spiritual" that the new person's relation to the congregation is poorly defined and lacks any accountability whatsoever.

A justification-based membership doesn't deny the right of church leaders to put biblical demands on people and to expect biblical responsibility. Some demands are biblical! For example, a church may biblically expect:

- *serving* (Rom. 12:1; Eph. 2:10)
- *controlling one's tongue* (1 Thess. 3)
- *tithing* (Gen. 14; Mal. 3)
- *demonstrating the fruit of the Spirit* (Gal. 5)
- *loving others and self* (1 Cor. 13; Col. 3:12-15)
- *attending worship* (Heb. 10:25; Acts 2:42–47)
- *caring specifically for the disadvantaged* (Matt. 25)

Membership, therefore, is spiritual, rooted in justification, and yet also demands some attention to practical process and biblical expectations. What should the process look like? The answer isn't found in a single Bible passage or in the traditions or policies of a particular church. The answer is rooted in justification but shaped by the *diversity* of people coming into the church.

Diversifying Church Membership

Not all people are the same and not all membership expectations should be identical. Justification is just, but the diversity of people demands that the church avoid a one-size-fits-all membership process. There will be some uniform patterns for membership, but these will be simple and affirming for people of all backgrounds (such as a coffee and tea some evening for all newcomers joining the church).

The following examples show how this type of justification-based thinking and acting might work practically. All the following are real examples about actual people.

Pondering Real Cases of Diverse Membership

Flower children from the 1970s. Hank and Viola in many ways never left the 1970s. They still wear headbands and like to cruise around in their restored Volkswagen minibus. They adore Jesus and they love people. They come to church every Sunday to serve where they can. But they don't want formal commitments. They're nervous about membership. "We love Jesus, but we don't like fancy rules," they openly say. They're happy to be called members as long the process is informal and unofficial. The church accepts them with little or no formal process, other than talking with them about their love of the Lord as their savior.

The successful businessman. Rich is in his early sixties and respects formal membership in organizations. He is a successful businessman, a Rotarian, a volunteer for United Way, and serves on several boards. Because he knows what formal membership in an organization often entails, he avoids church membership. Years ago he was an elder in a fine church. Then he went through a divorce. His fellow elders sided with his wife and severely disciplined him, including refusing to let him take communion for several months. Rich resigned from the elder board and the church, determined (in his mind) never to be similarly hurt again. He worships regularly at his new church, gives generously, and volunteers. The church records him as a member even though he declines to participate in any formal membership process.

The seasoned church couple. A couple has been Presbyterian for years. They move to a new city and become interested in a nondenominational church. After a year of regular worship attendance and some volunteer work, they decide to join. The pastor jovially tells them he knows how much they love the Lord and have already bonded with congregants. "As far as we're concerned, you are members and we'll leave it at that," says the pastor. The couple is taken aback. They're seasoned church people. They have membership papers in their former church. They expect classes, meetings with the church leaders, and a formal welcome on a Sunday morning. They expected much more than privately expressed good wishes. After listening to their disappointment, the pastor apologizes and quickly arranges for the "more."

The two contrasting teenagers. Two sixteen-year-old friends approach the pastor after morning worship, indicating they want to join the church together. The first one grew up in the church and attended nearly every Sunday school and catechism class offered. The second one is new to any church and recently accepted Christ. Does the pastor prepare each teen for membership in the same way? Probably not.

An unawares religious "liberal" and a thrice-married conservative. Winifred is fifty years old and just married for the third time after two nasty divorces linked to her drug and alcohol abuse. She grew up in a conservative church which she attended until her addictions drove her away. Her new husband was and still is a member of a very theologically liberal congregation that doesn't really preach the gospel. Both Winifred and her new husband respond to the pastor's biblical preaching and want to join the church. The husband simply desires to transfer his membership from the liberal congregation. Winifred hopes her former congregation will send her records from twenty-five years ago. They tell their new pastor that their papers are on the way and would like to schedule a Sunday morning to be welcomed. Should they be members by paper transfer? If not, why not? How should the pastor proceed? Why?

These real-life examples show that the church needs to be ready for diverse situations even if it's committed essentially to accepting newcomers based on their faith in Christ. Moreover, since the church must care for its members by building them up "in the Lord," every congregation should consider the many ways it could promote sanctification.

Nurturing Sanctification for all Members

Here are some ways church leaders can promote robust sanctification even while basing church base membership on justification:

- Establish a basic, minimal, biblical standard for membership based on justification—John 3:16—"Do you believe in Jesus as your own Savior and Lord?"
- Host a simple new-member meeting in which people gather with others who are also joining the church. Focus on getting to know each other and some leaders of the church as well as on learning things pertaining to the church, its teachings, and it's policies.
- Create a learning-and-giving culture that offers a diversity of enticing classes, mission opportunities, and volunteer possibilities. Joining such activities becomes part of the thinking and lifestyle of the church. The building becomes a busy place seven days a week.
- Fashion sermons to teach the veterans as well as the novices, including meaningful challenges to attendees to become involved in realistic opportunities for service.
- Welcome new members in a worship service after they have completed any expectations unique to their situation.

- Accept new members who resist formal involvements, personally welcoming them to the church by placing their names in the member directory and inviting them to meet informally with the pastor and other leaders.
- List in the church directory and member roster as "regular attendees" all people who regularly attend over a lengthy period of time (e.g., four to nine months) and who make obvious moves to be connected to the church in some way (Bible studies, volunteering, financial giving, etc.). Treat them like members. They receive mailings, hospital calls, funeral home visits, and invitations to join groups such as the choir. These invitations help them to feel part of the family and affirm their spiritual membership even if they haven't been officially received as full members.

These practices and others like them show people that the church cares and embraces them based on their faith in Christ—that justification naturally leads to sanctification. The practices provide some structure and process linked to peoples' diverse faith journeys and personal circumstances. Such a blend of faith and process avoids sending the message that membership depends purely on human, cultural invention. Such sensitive new-member thinking and acting lay the groundwork for new Christians' growth into a learning, living, and giving member of the Kingdom of God and God's church.

Discussion Questions

1. What do you think of Charles Colson's idea about congregants signing an agreement to give their time and money to a congregation before being able to become members?

2. Would it be practical and appropriate for a church to make it relatively easy to become a new member and then to provide an array of classes and activities for new members to grow in their faith? Would it be similar to minimizing pre-marital counseling but at the same time emphasizing classes and counseling after the wedding?

3. The chapter lists seven biblical demands for members. Based on your understanding of Scripture, are there more such demands that could be included on the list?

4. The second half of the chapter includes various examples of new-member quandaries. Do they suggest that there might be some merit in adapting the membership process for each person or couple? Explain.

14

Leading a Congregation Organically

A respected church member is willing to run for the position of elder. He is elected. His idea of being an elder is that he will pastor people, use his spiritual wisdom, and help oversee the maturity and spiritual strength of the congregation. Once on the elder board, however, he finds he is usually involved in long discussions on the state of the church building, the administration of the church, staff relations, various committee reports, denominational issues, and more.

Conversely, a woman accepts the role and label of elder and is eager to use her administrative gifts to bring order and structure to what she believes has been a sloppily-run organization. Instead, she is assigned hospital calls and pastoral discipline cases.

Which one of these two new elders is really serving as an elder? How does the church decide what an elder is and who should be one? When lines aren't clearly drawn and labels don't clearly define roles, frustration can result. Often people will even avoid serving in leadership because of mixed messages and uncertain assignments.

The governance of the modern church often shows strong parallels with business and industry. Both the church and business are committed to such things as order, efficiency, effective structuring, leadership, attention to the market, staff development, budgets, statistical trends, and growth.

The church, though, is unique in that its governance must be carefully blended with humane qualities such as love and compassion not especially expected and certainly not required in the secular world. Also, the church must carefully monitor the congregation's feelings and needs. The corporate world certainly does something similar with its customer base, but the awareness and reaction to leadership decisions in the church are often more immediate and intense. Business and industry can make many decisions, hire and fire people, change their method of operation, and alter their advertising methods, but many customers might not know or care. Congregants tend to be emotionally invested in their churches—especially the more involved members.

Church leaders will face angry and frustrated parishioners almost immediately if a staff member is fired or the methods of worship are changed. While the church has a business dimension, it's biblically structured and designed more like a family. The church family monitors church leadership and decision-making more closely than customers monitor the business world. Customers mainly want a quality product or service at a good price. Congregants want a quality "product" and a reasonable church budget, but they also expect harmony, peace, and faithfulness to God and each other in the church family.

Introducing Churches' Multiple Stakeholders

The church, then, is always balancing its business side with personal character and organizational values such as love, joy, peace, patience, kindness, goodness, gentleness, faithfulness, and self-control—the fruit of the Spirit. Church leaders must be very sensitive to expressed concern when decisions and changes are actually or potentially unpopular with or misunderstood by a congregation, especially when it generally appears that leaders acted wrongly. The church is a voluntary association that grows or declines according to the spiritually motivated good will of its members, not the sheer power of its leaders. Churches and even entire denominations can split over matters of ill will that years later seem so inconsequential. Moreover, leaders sometimes have to make unpopular decisions in order to be faithful to God to the best of their abilities. They serve God and the faithful, not a market per se. Church leaders are caretakers under God and on behalf of his followers. When God is a stakeholder, decision-making can be enormously complicated and humbling.

If church leaders care too much about efficiency, control, and statistically measurable success, the church may lose its vision of caring for people and its mission to minister to particular kinds of people. If a church overly focuses on the feelings of people, however, it risks having a poorly managed church that could fall apart because of both a lack of vision and unfocused organizational energy.

I'll never forget standing in the church parking lot one Sunday after worship with tearful church members who were also relatives of a man who had just been let go from the church staff. They and others in the church had demanded answers. But the answers were complex; the staff problems had developed over a long period of time. A full disclosure risked violations of privacy and could encourage legal action. The church leaders viewed the man's departure as the solution to a festering and frustrating employment issue. The family and friends of the man perceived their loved one being hurt by uncaring church leaders. They wondered how the leaders could be so insensitive. Potential divisiveness loomed in the congregation as people assumed that they needed to take sides.

Understanding Church as Formal Institution and Living Organism

To help analyze such complicated situations, I'll call the business, governance, and legal side of a church the church's *institution*. I'll call the feeling, familial, relational side of the church its *organism*.

The church as organism is a living, dynamic, relational body of believers in Jesus Christ. Even though this body has a building, a name, and often a denominational affiliation, it isn't fully defined by such structural and organizational things. This dynamic body has a unique energy. Its basic composition isn't legal, structural, or physical, but a spiritual unity in Jesus Christ. As I suggested earlier, there's a dynamic, mystical, invisible unity (1 Cor. 1, 3, 12; John 17; Eph. 4; 1 John). This strongly organic unity is rooted in such mysteries as voluntary love, affection, spirituality, prayer, and faith. Former Herman Miller CEO Max De Pree says in *Called to Serve: Creating and Nurturing the Effective Volunteer Board* that "structure is important but what's much more important—in fact, critical—is the willingness and ability of the people involved to establish and maintain amiable and productive relationships" (35). That's especially true of the church.

Nevertheless, a church also has an institutional side. The institution develops as the people in the organism need to find each other and gather together (a building and meeting schedules), to know how to worship with each other (liturgies, doctrines, music), and to function as a legal entity in the broader community (tax-exemption, by-laws, constitution, and board of leaders). At first, a church might be only a small group worshiping in someone's living room. The group grows, moves to a storefront, and eventually constructs its own building. Staff members need to be hired as the group expands, and decisions have to be made about children, youth, schedules, location, expenditures, and more. The simple organic unity becomes an institution, trying hard to hang on to its dynamic, organic identity. The institution and the organism—like rain and sun—need each other, always hoping for the rainbow.

There are rainbows, but the relational people and the institutional people often make each other nervous. Visionary pastors can make institutionally-oriented people uneasy. A pastor might have a great vision for growth, but someone has to make sure the building is adequate, the staff are trained, and the bills are paid. A very organized elder from a neighboring church once remarked to me, "Yeah, the pastor always has us working on some new-fangled vision statement or whatever you call it." A more institutionally minded pastor can damage the passion and joy of the organism. Zealous institutional people can dilute the passion for ministry, while ambitious, loving pastoral leaders can cause administrators to walk out the door frustrated, threatening to never come back until the church has its fiscal and organizational houses in order.

Balancing Institution and Organism

A congregation will be confused or even agitated if there isn't a fitting balance between the organism and the institution. Poorly managed congregations sow congregational mistrust. Churches excessively focused on formal management find some members fuming, "We're finely tuned, but just not very spiritual. We run a good business, but we've lost our first love." Seeking the proper balance is a way for a church to demonstrate its commitment to using the institution for the sake of fulfilling a working vision of caring for people. The institution has a greater mission than its own organizational and financial preservation.

Sometimes the balance between organism and institution is thrown off because of confusing labels. Labels have power. We use various leadership labels in the church: elder, deacon, trustee, board member, senior pastor, manager, administrator, director, and more. The label a person receives may not be clearly defined. The person holding the title might not even know if their work should be primarily organic/relational or institutional/organizational. Sometimes labels even cause such confusion. What is a "pastor of administration"—a pastor or an administrator?

Another consideration in appropriately balancing organism and institution is how church changes come about. Church leaders may view a change they institute as a good business decision. Passionate members of the congregation may see the decision and the resulting change as a sign of an unhealthy, controlling bureaucracy characterized by a failure to be led by the Spirit. Consistent worship liturgy might be viewed by institutional people as a sign of integrity and good order; they desire consistency from Sunday to Sunday and aren't extremely open to spontaneous changes in the worship flow. Other members, motivated by organic dynamics, will thirst for worship variety and more spontaneous, Spirit-led worship experiences. Staff change is yet another example. Removal of a non-productive or non-cooperative staff person will be welcomed by institutionally-minded leaders. Organically-minded leaders will grieve, announcing a lack of love and caring for the dismissed staff person; their disgust with church politics will grow.

Integrating Organism and Institution

To have a productive, happy, and peaceful church that can fulfill its commitment to the working vision of caring for people, church leaders must understand the dynamics of both the organism and the institution. Pastors, staff, and other church leaders must first accept the need for both the organism and the institution. The church secretary may love everybody, but too many mistakes in the church bulletin, too many dropped phone messages, and too many overlapped room schedules coupled with a loving smile can wear thin. The senior pastor may lead the board expertly, schedule visits diligently, and preach with pinpoint doctrinal accuracy. If the same pastor lacks passion for individual members, seems uncaring to staff, and rarely smiles in the pulpit, however, members will grow critical of the pastor—even if congregants don't say much publicly about their concerns. Good pastoring normally requires some good administration (How long did the very ill and worried Mabel have to wait for the pastor?), and good administrators must be Christ-like, caring shepherds.

Think of the church as a building with a transparent wall down the middle. One side of the wall represents the institution and the other side the organism. While standing on either side of the building you can see through the wall to the other side. There is a door in the wall. The sign on the one side of the door reads "institution," and the sign on the other side reads "organism." The door is never locked, but swings freely on hinges. Members and staff not only *see* both sides, but pass easily between them. Some church staff and volunteers spend more time on one or the other side. Some of them might even forget where the door is located or to look at what's happening on the other side. The working vision is well met when the organism sees to the needs of the institution and when the institution sees to the needs of the organism so that both sides are mutually strong and supportive.

Beyond the analogy of the swinging door, how can a church envision the governance of a balanced, institution-organism congregation? It's one thing to *say* that the institution and organism must work together to nurture the care for real people. It's quite another thing to create a system and social environment which nurtures such care-focused cooperation. For this cooperation to succeed, the traditional system and model of a board of elders or deacons is largely inadequate. As I will show in the next chapter, the traditional model of elders and deacons (and boards of trustees) can create a church that looks and acts too much like a medieval monarchy or a modern corporation. There are crucial, necessary differences between the church as organism and institution. Generally speaking, however, the existence of a traditional board of elders and deacons unhealthily perpetuates a church's institutional dynamics over its organic life. If a church creates a leadership environment that looks and acts solely like a traditional business institution, it will be difficult to find that harmonious balance between organism and institution needed to fulfill the working vision.

The medium is also a message, and function does follow form in organizations. If we form our church governances to look and act like business or government, our churches could become more institutional than organic. The result could be a well-run institution, but at the risk of damaging the organism. A new wineskin of church governance is needed to encourage religious passion, a biblical body, and dynamic organism—without sacrificing needed institutional order and practicality. The place to begin building the new wineskin of church governance is by developing fitting leadership that understands this dual nature of the modern church.

Discussion Questions

1. To what extent does your congregation honor the church as both institution and organism? Explain.

2. Can you think of situations in your church when congregants didn't understand or appreciate leaders' decisions? Did those decisions seem like church politics?

3. The chapter includes an example of a church beginning in someone's living room but eventually becoming an institution. How and why would this happen? Is it inevitable?

4. Discuss the concept of a transparent wall down the middle of a church with a swinging door that separates the organic and institutional parts of the church. What kind of personality and sensitivities do church leaders, including a senior pastor, need to have in order to honor the wall and the door?

15

Labeling Congregational Leaders

Sociologist Philip G. Zimbardo conducted a classic research experiment on the significance of labels. Zimbardo hired college students to play-act roles in a mock prison. Some students were called "prisoners" (and were locked up), while others played guards and administrators. Shortly, the students who were labeled "guards" acted out their role *as they interpreted its label*. Some students who were acting as prisoners actually grew frightened, intimidated, and were even released (often weeping) before the experiment was completed. Students took the labels so seriously that they seemed to become their assigned labels.

Church leadership involves the meaning, purpose, and effects of various labels. How should a should church define "pastor" or "elder"? Church governance includes various labels that can help or hinder the work of the congregation. Some labels focus on service—others on authority. Some sound more institutional or organic. Some seem more friendly, authoritative, biblical, and empowering. Many labels come with elaborate job descriptions that neither the leader nor the congregation might know about or understand. Labels matter because we often put them on like professional clothes so we can play the parts.

Leadership in church structure and governance is a key factor in a congregation fulfilling its goal of serving people. Leadership—when it comes from many congregants and especially from the Holy Spirit as well as the official leaders—is critical for the success of a church as both institution and organism. Leadership labels suggest promises and responsibilities and even accountability. This is why commissioning and ordaining church leaders is no small matter. Leadership is crucial for a congregation to experience joy as well as growth in all areas of its ministry.

Leadership expert and best-selling author John Maxwell says in *The 21 Indispensable Qualities of a Leader* that everything rises and falls with leadership. That might seem like a stretch for a voluntary association like a congregation. But the actual leadership necessary to sustain a healthy church might be provided by those who lack any official leadership labels. Churches do live or die based on people's positive or negative leadership. Poor leadership in the church as institution leads to administrative and financial problems. A lack of leadership in the church as organism leads to suspicion, frustration, and dissatisfaction among congregants and staff. Good organic and institutional leaders together can nurture a healthy church that truly cares for God's children.

Pastors and other church leaders will often have gifts favoring either the institutional or the organic side of the church. They'll tend to be better at either formal programs and processes or interpersonal relations. Good leaders who are passionate for the institution and its administration but don't understand the organism will produce a finely-tuned organization that could lack warmth and spiritual passion. Skilled leaders who are passionate for the organism but lack institutional gifts may develop vibrant relationships in a congregation that feels insecure and distrusts its leaders. Entropy ensues.

Cooperating as Diverse Leaders

The challenge, then, is to nurture pastors and other leaders with labels that match their gifts and their responsibilities. All leaders need to be committed to both institution and organism, and to be enthusiastically supporting one another in pursuing a healthy balance between the two. Cooperation and balance will facilitate a passionate congregation that trusts the integrity of its leaders while serving its members. But the balance involves using a variety of different gifts for the common good.

This balanced, mutual cooperation between institutional and organic leaders is not common in today's churches. My goal in this and subsequent chapters is to redesign church governance and leadership to produce a biblically-led church structure that balances institution and organism to help congregations fulfill their mission.

The major problem we find in churches today is that structure and governance frequently are modeled too strongly after industrial and civic bodies. This was probably not the intent of people such as the Protestant reformer John Calvin when they revived biblical teachings on church governance in order to engender more lay involvement and to distinguish such governance from the more professionalized Roman Catholic Church culture.

Today, industry-modeled congregations generally are led by boards, trustees, and CEOs. These churches depend on the work of hosts of committees and committee chairpersons. Such structuring often works in business partly because it expands the stakeholders and can bring into leadership more people with organic as well as institutional skills and sensibilities. But is such formal, highly institutional governance adequate for the church as a distinct kind of organism? How can the church develop a more diverse, less purely institutional-minded leadership without compromising its biblical commitments?

Institutional Leadership

A church often sets up a model of governance similar to industry, only with different names and titles. The board of trustees becomes the board of elders. The CFO and budget committee become the deacons. The CEO and chairperson of the board may be the senior pastor. Elders and deacons are assigned to standing committees and often become their committee chairpersons. Elder meetings are typically run like board meetings with committee reports and board decisions that get reported back to standing committees. The church staff—like company employees—are given their job assignments from that board and proceed in their work as directed by the board of elders. The biblical idea, then, of an elder-led congregation is somewhat similar to corporate management models. Of course leaders in both church and business can experience power struggles, politics, strained relations, and distrust.

Institutional church leadership models are evident in the power of particular labels. Church leaders often are very familiar with the labels and their meaning as found in industry. When a person is elected or appointed into a church governance position, the label (such as "elder") is associated with business leadership. "elder" and "senior minister" are interpreted as CEO, trustee, or president of the company. The church labels can carry with them the ideas of power, authority, and privilege that are found in much of the corporate world.

Powering Down Leadership Labels

Labels are extremely important in the corporate world partly because they signal how people should consider each other and work with one another. A person in a position of power also usually acts accordingly. I once asked a wealthy business owner where he would like to go with me to lunch. He responded that he eats only in his own, personal dining room at the corporate offices, where he has his own chef. I met him there.

On the other hand, people who have so-called menial jobs often have to use labels that signal little or no prestige and power: dishwasher, floor scrubber, janitor, and seed planter. Sometimes businesses enhance the prestige and even power of employees simply by changing their labels. The high school person who puts food on hospital trays is called an "assistant nutritionist." The dishwasher serves as a "sanitation engineer." The seed planter becomes the "greenhouse plant supervisor." The bank teller is dubbed a "customer service representative." Labels can suggest standing as well as tasks and responsibilities.

Industry, business, and governmental bodies frequently use power and prestige labels—and that's often fine for their purposes. When churches use such labels for governance, however, problems can easily occur because people tend to act out the meaning of their perceptions of their label. As I said, labels are like uniforms. An industrial mentality, which often promotes power, prestige, and privilege, replaces biblical models of servant leadership, Spirit-led leadership, gifts of the Holy Spirit, and a focus on love and unity in the familial body of Christ.

Avoiding Leadership Power Plays

I remember attending a conference led by a church management expert. In one of the sessions, the expert lectured on how the pastor can and should relate to the church board and the individual board elders. For two hours he explained how to work within a system he characterized as "power moves" and "hidden agendas." One of the things to watch for, he said, is the probability that some board decisions will be driven by board members' spouses, who give male board members an earful at dinner before board meetings.

He also said that pastors must identify the "power people" on the board and determine how to work with them behind the scenes before important meetings occur in order to be more certain that a needed decision will go the "right" way—that *pastor's* way.

I felt like I was learning how to become a junior state legislator or even a lower-level executive in a somewhat dysfunctional corporation. I wasn't learning how to be a shepherd—a servant. I wasn't learning about promises and responsibilities to others. This conference speaker was not a burned-out ex-minister merely releasing pent-up anger. He was a nationally known church expert, author, and popular speaker. He had plenty of power-signifying labels to his credit. The sad thing was that he was probably accurately describing how to be a successful pastor in a dysfunctional church institution. He just assumed all churches wanted to be like the one described in his case study.

Considering Real Power Play Examples

When fine members of a congregation are voted into or appointed to office, some will naturally adopt the labels of power and prestige that they learned in business or government. They probably won't fully understand the organic dynamics of the church. I've experienced such misunderstanding in many real-life situations.

Parents lobby for adolescents. Passionate parents and an excited youth pastor visit the church leaders at a Monday-evening meeting, seeking permission to send a group of thirty youth on a two-week mission trip, including a three-day outdoor Christian music festival. The leaders indicate that the request hasn't come through committee channels but still agree to hear the request. After listening to the parents and youth pastor, leaders express concerns that the trip is expensive and that they don't know the nature of the outdoor festival. The leaders thank them for coming and promise they will discuss it, refer it to committee, and report back. The visitors leave a bit deflated but moderately hopeful. Several weeks pass as the parents and youth leaders grow anxious. Finally, a phone call to the youth pastor reports that the request is honorable but the leaders have decided they should wait a year to determine precise funding and explore the real nature of the music festival. The parents, youth pastor, and youth are fuming.

The unacceptable firing. Church leaders meet to discuss whether a repeatedly irresponsible staff member must be terminated. During the leaders' discussion, there's a knock on the door. Several church members inform the leaders that many congregants have gathered in a room down the hall to pray "for the Spirit's leading and for the board to realize how precious this staff person is to them." Several leaders are confused and annoyed. The spontaneous prayer meeting, they believe, is inappropriate and shows a lack of respect for the authority of the leaders. Leaders make no contact with the church members. The board votes to dismiss the staff person and leaves the building while congregants continue praying.

Families complain about a lazy pastor. A note is sent to the senior pastor asking for it to be read at that evening's board meeting. The missive is from three church families complaining that the pastor hasn't been calling on the shut-ins. The pastor, though not on leave or vacation, indeed hasn't attended to his calling duties even though several visiting preachers replaced him on Sundays. The leaders discuss the note briefly and then ask the clerk of the board to write a response to the families, informing them that the pastor has been deeply involved in administrative and financial sessions related to end-of-the-year planning, and that the pastor will return to his normal routine as soon as the new year begins.

In each of these three situations, the leaders aren't bad people. Institutionally speaking, they aren't totally inept leaders. In each situation, however, they fail to connect with the hearts of the people. They forget to consider their churches' unique balance between institution and organism. Each situation demonstrates how their actual working vision isn't focused on caring for people as much as on following institutional procedures and maintaining leadership authority.

The waiting children's ministry leaders. A children's ministry staff and volunteers passionately care about kids. The staff develop plans for their department, believing such plans will best serve the children. They're informed that they must submit their plans to the full board for approval. The plans come to the board, but since the board members aren't at church every day, they neither fully understand the plans nor relate to the passion and vision of the ministry's enthusiastic staff. The board's agenda is very full that night, so members decide to table the children's-ministry proposal. The children's-ministry leaders are frustrated since they had hoped to implement their ideas immediately. They're forced to wait.

The next month the proposal goes before the board. Now, however, with more time to address the proposal, the board picks it apart. Then the board quickly designs its own proposal from scratch. Ironically, board members don't fully support their own new proposal. After an hour's discussion, the board decides to set up a committee to come up with a recommendation. The children's leaders are now enormously frustrated. They realize that by the time a proposal is (they hope) accepted it may well be unacceptable to them, and that several months will have passed before they could even begin implementation.

The problem in this example is that board members are too far removed from daily ministry and can't begin to fully understand and appreciate the ideas, practices, and passion of the church staff and leaders. The board's reaction to the children's ministry proposal follows an organizational rather than organic model. The people in the trenches feel defeated. They're just about ready to resign. If the board wants to dictate how the children's ministry works, the ministry team reasons, let the board do the actual ministry work itself.

Many existing models of church governance certainly have biblical elements, such as elders, deacons, good order, and authority. But sometimes the governance structure itself and the overall effects of the structure aren't biblical. The existing church structures don't have room for key biblical norms, such as being Spirit led, using God-given gifts, and joyfully experiencing a fitting balance between institution and organism. Most churches need to develop a model of governance that is significantly more people focused and decentralized.

The goal of good governance should not be how one side (institution or organism) can dominate the other. Rather, a proper goal is to determine how each side can seamlessly serve the other side. Churches need an institutional model that actually draws volunteers into the work of both the institution and the organism and gives the people in the trenches more authority to serve others as they see fit. Churches require a structure that provides sound administration, but also promotes joy, service, and unity. As I will illustrate in the next chapter, the biblical model exists—and it will work for most churches

Discussion Questions

1. Discuss, with respect to your church, John Maxwell's idea that that everything rises and falls with leadership.
2. Is your church governance at all like business management? How? Is this right and appropriate for your congregation? Explain.
3. How do labels give power and prestige where you work or volunteer? How do they do so in your church? Are there any better labels that your church might use to define its leaders?
4. The second half of the chapter offers examples of members annoyed and even hurt by church leadership decisions. Are they realistic examples? Could they happen in your church? Why or why not?

16

Leading Churches Vertically

Years ago I visited a childhood friend living in a different city. He took me on a guided tour, including of the church where he had become a member. "I'll be an elder starting next September," he said. I congratulated him and then asked when he had been elected. "The election's next month," he replied. "How do you know you'll be elected?" I wondered out loud. I still recall his answer: "There are three elder positions to fill, but only two of us agreed to put our names into nomination. I'm basically already elected. Our church has a hard time finding willing elders."

Recently I visited a cousin and his wife. He told me he had just been appointed elder in his Lutheran church. "They must be desperate," spouted his wife. My cousin agreed. "No one else would do it so I said I would as long as I could be gone all summer at our cottage. They agreed, so now I'm an elder."

Why do some churches have so much difficulty getting people to serve?

Overcoming Congregational Resistance to Service

One problem is churches whose governance is based on a stereotypical corporate model with little influence from biblical insights about leadership and church organization. Some church leaders, especially those without significant business experience, do believe that this simplistic corporate model of management is necessarily appropriate and effective for every church. But even many business leaders realize its inappropriateness. Why should a savvy business leader voluntarily serve a church whose governance structure doesn't fully fit the purpose of the church?

Moreover, many congregants accept the tension, stress, and poor time management in church leadership because they experience and expect such problems in their daily work environments. Of course church leaders would prefer to avoid time-consuming meetings, awkward phone calls, stressful decisions, feelings of inadequacy, and endless congregational politics. They would like their church experience to reflect peace, joy, learning, and growing. But they often don't learn even in business, government, or education the attitudes and skills needed for church leadership. They don't normally learn soft skills such as caring for others.

So two things happen in the church. First, gifted and experienced leaders often refuse to serve because they don't want the added aggravation in their lives. Second, those who love church governance and really want to serve frequently have their own agendas and even enjoy the same power, control, and discipline that sometimes threaten the mood and joy of serving the church as a special, living organism.

Recognizing the Institutional Roots of Contemporary Churches

The move to a more top-down, control-oriented model of church governance began earnestly after World War II, but it has roots all the way back to the ancient Roman empire during the second and third centuries of the Christian church. The first century church (Pentecost–AD 100) was "charismatic." Congregations were led by Spirit-filled people who expressed and used the unique gifts of the Spirit. When the apostle Paul writes some of his earliest letters to churches (e.g., 1 Cor.), he doesn't appeal to a hierarchical structure of elders to solve the obvious problems. He appeals to a spirit of unity and advises emerging congregations to work together and to discipline each other based on their gifts (1 Cor. 12). As the church entered the second and third centuries, it began shifting from a more Spirit-led, gift-driven model to a more formal organization patterned loosely after the Roman city-state.

Large cities such as Rome modeled how many believers then assumed the church ought to be structured. After all, at that time civic government was the major source for organizational structures and processes, just as corporate structures and processes dominate today's thought about how organizations of all kinds should function. Church leaders interpreted the Greek *presbyteroi* (elders) in the context of the Roman senate, and *episcopos* (bishop) in terms of the Roman emperor. The bishop was increasingly viewed as inheriting apostolic authority (apostolic succession). The writings of church fathers of the second and third centuries called for people to revere and obey the bishops just as Roman citizens venerated the emperor.

The actual biblical terms for leadership in the early first-century church don't seem to express such hierarchical structure. The *presbyteroi* may well have been wise, older people (the word means "older") who gave wisdom to the body of believers. The *episcopos* (overseer) may have been only someone with gifts of leadership and administration who helped to oversee the activities of the church; they probably were gifted pastorally as well as administratively.

As the church moved into the second and third centuries, it may have needed a more sharply-defined, hierarchical form of governance. Heresies and persecutions abounded. Strong leadership probably helped the church through many difficult days. The gathering of bishops at Nicaea in 325 to hammer out doctrinal issues illustrates how God used strong leaders to form and protect biblical truth during theologically and ecclesiastically turbulent years.

Reforming the Church

As centuries passed, however, increasingly rigid and hierarchical forms of church governance often burdened people and congregations. Competition among leaders, struggles for power, and corruption in high places sometimes threatened even the existence of the church. The medieval church was fraught with intrigue, competition, war, hatred, and immorality among bishops and popes. The 16th-century Reformation, which began centuries before, was partly a rebellion against the corruption and hierarchical power the church leaders held over the common people, who were sometimes even spiritually abused. The Reformation's doctrine of "faith alone" was partly a return to the individual's freedom of faith and conscience in their personal relationships with their God.

But the Reformation didn't eliminate the hierarchical structures of most churches. Church governance was still tied to civic government, so people's lives and conscience remained partly under the domination of allied church and civic leaders. The emerging Protestant groups were often just as eager as their medieval church governance ancestors to persecute and even kill those who disagreed with accepted doctrines (e.g., Calvinists killed Anabaptists).

Accepting the Need for Contemporary Church Governance

In fact, today's churches still inherent elements of governance models from the second century, the Middle Ages, and even the Reformation—as well as from post-World War II corporate settings. Many churches imagine biblical church governance as the process of asserting top-to-bottom control over congregations.

Power and authority, of course, aren't bad. They're biblical. The Bible calls for strength in leadership from the days of Judge Deborah to the apostle Peter. The authority given to parents is often seen as a model of how God created authority and obedience. We're are all subject to Christ and his Word. Obedience is no stranger to the Christian's life. The question for churches today isn't whether or not they require leadership and authority. The real question is how leadership and authority are labeled, defined, and practiced.

For instance, vertical authority is top-down authority. Attention is given to how elevated a person is in the vertical line of command. The focus is a leader's position in the vertical structure. The higher the position, the greater the power. Labels create names and titles to define and describe positions and accompanying levels of prestige and power. Some churches even create elaborate flow charts to illustrate positions and accompanying powers "over" those people situated lower in the chart.

Evaluating the Values of Vertical Positioning

Such vertical positioning isn't necessarily bad. It's probably good and necessary in large, complex organizations such as governments and corporations. Members of small groups such as families even need to know where they fit; children should obey their parents, and spouses need to build up and serve each other in the Lord. But the early first-century church didn't think in terms of elaborate vertical hierarchies. Neither did it think in terms of positions such as board members, board presidents, trustees, bishops, and archbishops.

Strictly vertical church governance appears to be more of a human invention than a biblical mandate. Moreover, it may not be healthy for most congregations. Such structuring emphasizes the institution and might weaken the energy and passion of the organism, locking the interior door between the church institution and organism. When the joy of the organism wanes and leadership becomes a burden, the working vision of caring for people suffers. Then even leaders are poorly served.

Nevertheless, vertical authority structures work well in some churches. These vertically governed churches run smoothly, and many Spirit-filled believers are eager to lead. Politics are minimal and the organism is healthy—even with strong, strictly vertical governance. Sometimes this style of governance simply works for a given congregation at a particular time and place.

Admitting the Limits of Vertical Governance

In many congregations where the spiritual fire is gone, however, leaders and staff are highly stressed, joyless, and unwilling to serve. If such congregations have only tried more of the same vertical power structure, it's time to try something new, especially a more openly biblical approach that might reignite the entire congregation and renew the efforts of disappointed or cynical leaders and other members.

These burned-out congregations often appear successful to outsiders, but morale is usually low and different factions often seek to push the church in conflicting directions. Worship and Sunday school attendance, financial giving, formal baptisms and weddings, and sanctuary size hardly guarantee a vibrant congregation.

Also, what about individual leaders in such a seemingly successful church? The church may appear successful while damaging individuals who move into vertical power positions. Beneath the surface are burnout, disillusionment, and frustration. When a member retires from office, they feel personally worn out and emotionally drained; they're not inclined to serve again. They're relieved their term is over, but their negative emotions will continue. They're far more likely to become a disparaging member who gossips about the problems in their church's governance.

No governance model will solve all the problems brought up in this chapter, or even all of the issues experienced by the retiring members described above. But a more flexible biblical model can help a church to realize a better balance between the institution and organism as it pursues a working model of caring for people. That biblical model exists. The model employees horizontal rather than vertical governance.

Discussion Questions

1. Do churches normally have difficulty finding people to accept key leadership positions such as elder and deacon? Has your church had such difficulties? If so, why?

2. How did the ancient churches tend to pattern governance after the Roman city-states? Does that development help explain the transformation of church leaders into bishops and the papacy?

3. What are examples of when or where vertical authority is necessary in society and families?

4. Can you think of ways that vertical authority in congregations today could be beneficial but also harmful?

17

Leading Churches Horizontally

Eighty-year-old Rich has been a jail chaplain for over thirty years. If you interviewed Rich for that job, you probably wouldn't hire him. He doesn't seem to have the normal talents needed to work with young men in a county jail. Thirty years ago, Rich just seemed to stumble into this work. But for many years God has used Rich to effectively minister to young inmates in his community. Rich simply does great work—almost by instinct.

God gives humans gifts for service. When the gift is present, the job will likely get done and the worker will experience great joy. Often the spirit prods people into service that they themselves don't feel fully confident to perform.

The biblical model for church governance and leadership evident in the early church is a horizontal structure rooted in gifts and calling rather than in positions and power. The most popular model of church governance today is probably based on corporate and governmental practices and is considerably more vertically structured than the organic church model I discuss in this chapter. Figure 1 captures the type of vertical governance typical today in most churches with two hundred or more members. Smaller churches frequently maintain the same type of governance. Generally speaking, the larger the church the more vertical the structure, perhaps even with four or five levels of people reporting "up" to those above them in the church governance hierarchy.

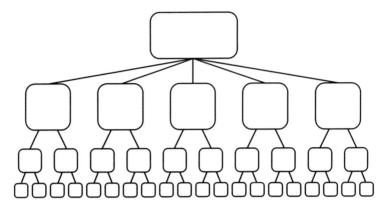

figure 1. An example of vertical church governance.

In contrast, figure 2 illustrates a more horizontal governance structure with less bureaucracy and greater shared power and authority. It also assumes freedom for consultation among all involved. The large rectangle represents the fact that all of the people are "in Christ." Jesus holds the church together and gives life to all congregants.

The focus in horizontal governance is collaboration, not control. Horizontal governance emphasizes delegated authority so that those who are called, gifted, and equipped to do their work are not repeatedly second-guessed from those "above," or simply told what to do by the higher-ups.

Horizontal governance and authority promote the idea that all people—all of whom are leaders within their own areas—of the church are basically equal and that authority should be fittingly decentralized. Whatever power leaders possess is linked primarily to their gifts and callings, not to their vertical or hierarchical position. The children's ministry director, for example, has some authority in their area of children's ministry. But this director makes significant decisions with the people who assist her. Her authority isn't "positional" as much as collaborative. The director and her assistants make decisions for the department as they see fit; they aren't bound to the approval of boards, elders, or deacons in authority above her. The boundaries for the director are the rights and privileges of the other ministries and directors around them who

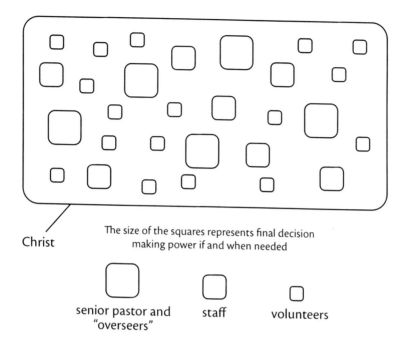

Christ

The size of the squares represents final decision making power if and when needed

senior pastor and "overseers"   staff   volunteers

figure 2. An example of horizontal church governance.

have power and authority in their areas rooted in their own unique gifts and callings. *Ultimately* the director is accountable to any designated pastor in the congregation, but *practically* is in charge of their own ministry on behalf of the congregation.

Establishing Horizontal Governance

Horizontal structuring and decentralized authority begin with the church asking what the Bible demands of all congregations and what needs and opportunities are uniquely expressed for that congregation in its mission statement. Once these things are determined, the church seeks the people with the gifts and calling who can carry out the demands and meet the goals of these opportunities. Vertical governance generally begins with, and is subsequently focused on, the traditional positions that need to be filled. Horizontal governance begins with identifying church needs.

As I explained earlier, in order to be successful, horizontal governance requires each congregation to dedicate time for asking critical questions about its own needs and self-identity. This process is basically the same as developing a mission statement. It's essential for horizontal governance. The questions might include:

- Who are we?
- What does the Bible demand of us—such as preaching, teaching, guiding, and witnessing?
- What unique opportunities do we have, given our make-up, location, and interests?
- What are nearby churches doing well that we might not need to do?
- What are nearby churches doing poorly that we might do better?

While asking such questions, the church consults the working vision of caring for people. The church doesn't merely assume, "We must teach. Let's find a teacher." Rather, the church examines itself to see who the people are that need to be taught and what they need to learn. Then it considers who has the gifts and calling to teach particular kinds of people. When the congregation identifies such a willing and gifted person in its midst, that person is called and granted authority to conduct that ministry. They're subject only to the boundaries of other staff people, directors, and volunteers who are ministering alongside of them and who are all holding themselves accountable to each other.

Receiving Gifts and Callings

The church, then, anchors authority in gifts and callings related to the specific needs and goals defined by the church. No one leads a church-sanctioned ministry unless they're gifted for that ministry and they believe they're called to that ministry. Gone are the days of begging from the pulpit or in the bulletin for needed volunteers. Instead, specific people are presented with the ministries. The people are then challenged to: (1) listen to God to discern if they're being called personally for the ministry, and (2) to consider the fact that if they truly are called then God has given or will give them the gifts for that ministry.

Vertical governance asks, "What positions need to be filled?" Horizontal authority structuring says, "We have identified ministry that needs to be done as part of our particular mission. Who has the gifts to lead and accomplish such ministry? Who is being called?" The difference may seem a bit nitpicky, but it's considerable. Are people called just to fill positions or in response to God's call and the call of the church to practice specific ministry? Even when it comes to "hiring" a pastor, the congregational identification of need (or "mission") and the subsequent talk with candidates about calling have been hijacked by the language of positions and authority. Frequently the result is that pastors end up doing things that were not included in the official job description because the description itself was based originally on what leaders thought the pastor should do rather than what needed to be done to fulfill the church's mission.

Who defines each ministry and seeks the gifted people? Certainly the pastor and others who know the church and the congregation's needs. Most of the planning and the search for workers, however, is done by the people in the individual departments or ministries. This isn't the work of boards or committees. The individual ministry directors know best what needs to be done, how to do it, and what sorts of people are needed. These chosen people connect with those in the congregation; they most likely have the calling and gifts to meet the needs identified by the church community.

When ministry leaders are given the freedom and authority to envision, shape, plan, and execute their own ministries, burnout is low. Excited leaders do what they know and believe is best without waiting for boards or committees to decide and approve. Each ministry leader serves in their trench and holds *trench authority*. The hands-on, spontaneous ministry done by gifted, called people generates enthusiasm and passion. While the overall identification of church ministries is accomplished with the approval of church leaders and is articulated in the congregation's own mission statement, the specific approaches to the ministries are in the hands of those who are called and gifted to serve.

The calling process is not willy-nilly. A church shouldn't call leaders who are enthusiastic but who might end up doing their own thing, bankrupting the church, irritating the congregation, frustrating other leaders, and discouraging the congregants who are supposedly being served. Fortunately, leaders with trench authority are not only enthusiastic and passionate, but also gifted and judicious. Many will already have experience but haven't served because they simply weren't encouraged to consider the work as a calling. They're aware they're working side-by-side with other equally passionate and gifted leaders in other church ministries. The team must live in harmony by respecting the limits and boundaries inherent in the presence of other equally committed and hard-working directors.

Also, the ministry directors are seeking to serve the congregants and community according to the church's working vision. Therefore, they're motivated to offer programming that will bring out the most people and generate the greatest enthusiasm. Each ministry director has a budget and processes in place for spending money. People work freely, independently, side-by-side with natural rather than arbitrarily imposed boundaries. With adequate congregational vision and support, this system works.

Gifts and calling are crucial to make this model work. Gifts are exactly what the Bible calls for when describing how work ought to be done in the church. It's important in horizontal governance to understand the difference between gifts and talents. A talent is something people are born with, such as musical ability, a way with words, or artistic flair. We often work and study to develop and refine our talents. Talent is important, but unique gifts are the heart of ministry (1 Cor. 12; Eph. 4). A gift is a special empowerment from God to meet a particular need and achieve a specific goal in the Kingdom. Gifts are the work of the Holy Spirit. God can use a person's talent by gifting that person for a specific calling. While the Spirit may use a person's talent, often people even with undeveloped talents will be gifted by the Spirit to do and achieve what the church and the Kingdom need at a particular time and place.

Reviewing Real Examples of Gifts and Callings in Action

From day laborer to Sunday school teacher. My father was never trained to be a teacher and had no experience working with children or youth. Yet there was a need in the congregation for a Sunday-school teacher, and he felt called. He nervously submitted his name, and when accepted for service he suddenly changed. Normally only a day laborer—punching in and punching out—he suddenly displayed a creative side no one had seen before. He established a unique place for the class (in the bell tower), gave the class a special name, and engaged the kids in interesting ways. The result was a ministry that spanned at least twenty years, successfully training an entire generation of young people.

Along with gifts is the power of calling. A person must not only seek the gift(s) to do a certain work, but must also be called by God to do that work. Calling is somewhat objective because it can be very emotionally and spiritually tangible.

Calling is both inner and outer. The outer calling is the announcement in the church bulletin, the comment from the pulpit or, most importantly, the personal invitation from the ministry director who sees potential in a person. The inner calling is the voice, feeling, drive, desire, pull, or nagging in a person's inner being put there by the Spirit, drawing the person to the ministry in conjunction with an outer calling.

From garbage entrepreneur to worship arts director. One of our members has been a garbage collector for many years. He built up his private garbage business from scratch and in his thirties sold the greatly-developed business to a giant refuse corporation. The sale left him financially comfortable but restless. When we met to talk, he asked, "What does a man in his thirties do with the rest of his life?" I knew he loved music and was a successful business leader. We needed a music director at the time and I risked putting that challenge in front of him. He had never been a church music director. But he felt a call—the leading of the Spirit—that he couldn't deny. He accepted, believing that God would give the gifts needed to transition from the garbage business to worship music. The former garbage collector took a faltering music ministry and built it into a thriving arts department with over one-hundred volunteers, a variety of specialty groups, meaningful weekly worship, and many annual presentations in the church and to the wider community.

Celebrating Signs and Wonders

The music and arts leader came to recognize the importance of gifts and calling. He saw this not only in his own life, but also among the arts volunteers. He soon saw the difference between undirected talent and talent driven by the Spirit's gifts. He tells me that some volunteers wrongly need the spotlight and foolishly want their own agendas served. They have the talent, but don't understand the need to humble themselves and use their talent as a gift to bless the church. Such humility, along with a commitment to blessing others, comes only when the talented person is touched by the Spirit; then the talent becomes giftedness. Such gifted people understand teamwork and the need to share the spotlight. If someone comes to our arts and music director frustrated because they didn't get the solo part or they have not had the lead role often enough, he reminds them what the ministry is all about. They're shown the need to use gifts to serve people and to glorify God. If that doesn't work, they're encouraged to consider another calling within the church.

Understanding gifts and callings leads to expecting *signs and wonders* (Acts 2:42–47). Signs and wonders give credibility to the church's work. They occur when gifted people do what they believe God is calling them and gifting them to do. Such people touch and transform lives, accomplish unexpected things, achieve amazing goals, bless the church, and reveal the power of the Spirit to the community. Signs and wonders are evident as members:

- lift up people from the pit of despair and hopelessness (Ps. 103)
- help the spiritually blind to identify and heal the brokenhearted (Isa. 61)
- show people their sins are forgiven (James 5)
- help to heal people from their addictions (James 5)
- equip people to live in unity with God and others (John 17)
- witness nonbelievers come to Christ through the church (Acts 2:42–47)
- realize that neighborhoods are being improved because the church is the light of the world and the salt of the earth (Matt. 5)

When people are called by God and gifted by the Spirit, they learn to expect that great things will occur, and to work for such wonderful occurrences. Change *does* happen in peoples' lives. The Kingdom *does* come.

Can such passion and results occur in a church with vertical governance? Of course. Governance models don't themselves produce God's blessings. God does. God has, however, given us direction on how to construct empowering models through which he can and does work. In a biblical model, people are free and encouraged to listen for their own calling to use their gifts in an atmosphere that respects their trench authority.

Discussion Questions

1. Examine the church governance charts at the beginning of the chapter. What are the key characteristics and differences of the two charts? Which one is closer to the way your congregation operates?
2. Do you think it's possible that churches overemphasize job positions/descriptions while not adequately considering calling and giftedness? What about in your congregation?
3. How would you answer on behalf of your church the bulleted questions in this chapter? Does answering them help you see more clearly what your church is or should be doing?
4. What is *trench authority*—and how does it or should it relate to gifts, calling, signs, and wonders in your church?

18

Avoiding Burnout

Focusing on gifts and callings in a horizontal leadership model is one biblical approach to church governance. Gifts and calling are routes to nurturing passionate, servant-hearted people. They can also help prevent burnout.

Burnout among staff and volunteers can be a huge problem in churches. Burnout is characterized by physical and emotional fatigue. The primary sign of burnout is a depressed feeling in the pit of our insides—a feeling that hits when it's time to leave the house for the church, a sensation that overwhelms when it's time to prepare for what we've promised others we would do. Burnout is the lack of desire to continue doing what we once thought we really wanted to do. Burnout is the lack of motivation to continue a commitment that once brought joy.

Burnout is serious not only because a staff person or volunteer wants to give up a task, but also because the person begins to feel a desire to step away from every aspect of church life. Just entering the building elicits stress. The building has an uncomfortable aura. Such emotions threaten friendships, joy, worship, and even faith itself. We don't want staff people and volunteers to self-destruct. We want people to stay fresh, committed, excited, focused, and involved.

The problem of burnout can be especially bad for small congregations when only a handful of people need to do everything. This may be easier to avoid in large congregations where there are more people to share the load.

Extinguishing Passion

The guardian against burnout is *passion*. When people have passion for their work they stay excited and are more resistant to burnout. Passion is love for the work; a desire to "be there"; a sense of being needed; a strong realization of God's calling; a belief that one's gifts are making a difference in God's Kingdom. A passionate person has the intensity and determination to make things happen. A passionate person can't *not* be there. A passionate person wants to be part of the effort as well as the success of the church.

Vertical governance in some churches produces passionate, fulfilled staff and volunteers. But it also can create burnout when people feel unnoticed and unappreciated—like pawns in the bureaucratic structure. When congregants' ideas and dreams are buried in committees and board discussions, people tend to give up. Their fire goes out. Horizontal governance offers an alternative that can revive congregational passion and re-integrate burned-out people into meaningful service.

Reaping the Benefits Of Horizontal Governance

Horizontal church governance encourages real passion from the bottom up. People do what they feel called and gifted to do in a congregational environment that links dreams, ideas, and visions to concrete actions. Congregants feel free to act upon their dreams and visions. When church workers are needed in vertical governance, leaders often announce the need with a touch of guilt. In horizontal governance, excited leaders are empowered to find their own, capable volunteers based on their knowledge of people in the congregation. The excited leaders infect their workers with enthusiasm. Leader's enthusiasm draws to them gifted workers who want to be part of the action.

Horizontal governance empowers people to be creative and to accept power for the sake of others. Workers aren't burdened with committees, committee reports, board discussions, and ever-delayed board decisions. Gifted leaders are encouraged to make their own decisions and to efficiently carry out those decisions in their own timeframe. The people in the trenches carry their own authority. With trench authority come freedom, efficiency, spontaneity, creativity, and passion.

Horizontal governance links passion to gifts. When people act according to their gifts, they're fulfilled in their work (1 Cor. 12; Eph. 4). When they're performing outside the area of their gifts, they burn out. When people work in a positive and passionate environment, they're internally motivated to look within themselves and to honestly explore their own gifts. They grow excited about their potential, believing in themselves and the gifts God has given them. They develop a new confidence that produces and maintains passion.

Calling nurtures passion. In order to truly be effective in church work, volunteers must believe they're filling a true need created by God. They must feel the call, the push and pull of God's Spirit. They must see God moving in the church and witness how their own lives are fitting with God's plans. Passionate people love to recall how things just came together in God's timing to open the door for them serve. They love to tell of the phone call inviting them to serve at the very time they were praying for guidance. They tell of the bulletin announcement that hit them between the eyes the very Sunday they planned to stay home, but attended church anyway. They love to share how they ended up serving the church because they happened to bump into a church leader who needed their service.

This creative, free environment may be threatening and unacceptable to experienced church leaders. It may appear to lack proper controls and authority. Leaders may rightly wonder to whom these trench-authority leaders and volunteers are accountable. Does everyone just do as they please? It sounds like anarchy if not a ticket to mediocrity or even failure. Who determines whether or not such people are really contributing to the distinct mission of the church?

Setting Boundaries in Horizontal Governance

Properly developed horizontal governance provides important parameters, boundaries, and supervision. The horizontal concept creates shared supervision, positive peer pressure, and openness to new ideas and people. Such shared efforts practically guarantee that if a ministry is failing some people will speak up—often because the workers themselves don't even show up. Shared supervision and peer pressure are all about the leaders keeping watch over their ministries and the church in general. They're in the best position to supervise each other. They're the people who are in the building regularly because they feel passionately called and gifted to carry out their work. No one would dare do anything to threaten their partners' ministries or the church's mission.

Still, shared supervision works only when there is an openness and opportunity to express ideas and concerns. Staff persons need to be encouraged to lovingly confront each other and to bring difficult matters to gifted problem-solvers for resolution. Those gifted in problem solving normally will be the pastoral leaders of the church. These aren't simply board members or bosses, but people gifted with wisdom to help resolve problems when daily interactions are insufficient for resolution. Here again, the emphasis is on rapid and efficient action. Hurt feelings aren't buried with staff people. Volunteers aren't obsessing over mistakes or inadequacies. Problems are addressed quickly by those who work in the trenches.

There are risks in moving toward a horizontal governance. The horizontal church will lack the crisp outer look of a finely-organized and well-run organization. It will be a bit difficult at times to describe leadership, authority, and the processes by which things get done. Yet, this is church, not industry or civic government. When the church is filled with happy and passionate workers, the job gets done well and joyfully. The mission is addressed efficiently and responsibly by those in the trenches. The working vision of caring for people is realized. Burnout is low. God is praised.

Discussion Questions

1. How and why have you experienced burnout? Does the chapter describe it in a way that matches how you've experienced it? Explain.
2. How and why have you experienced great joy in church-related work? Is such joy common for members of your congregation? Why or why not?
3. How is horizontal governance linked to gifts, calling, and passion?
4. What kinds of boundaries are needed for horizontal governance to work in a church? Would this type of governance and boundary system work in your congregation?

19

Selecting Wise Leaders

orizontal governance doesn't focus on ascending and descending authority. Biblically speaking, wise believers (*presbyteroi/episcopoi*) do have shepherding roles "over" others, but the emphasis is less on exercising power than on overseeing, guiding, and serving the flock and its leaders. This model affirms biblical authority (1 Tim.; Titus). It also affirms that the power and authority of church leaders is a *promise* and a *responsibility*. When someone agrees to serve in leadership, that person and the rest of the leadership team promise to serve each other toward the church's common vision and mission. They also agree themselves to be responsible and to hold each other responsible for their respective work.

How should a congregation's leaders (ruling elders) lead if not by managerial and executive authority? From a leadership and organizational perspective, what is distinctive about the biblical mandate of shepherds leading God's people (Ezek. 34)? I suggest in this chapter that although all churches and secular organizations share some characteristics as human institutions, the church is called to practice leadership and exercise authority in distinctively biblical ways resembling horizontal governance.

Discovering the Real Role of Church Elders

As I mentioned, the two most important words in church leadership are *presbyteros* and *episcopos*. These Greek words are usually translated as "elder" and "bishop," respectively. *Presbyteros* refers to an older, wiser person who gives guidance, counsel, and direction. *Episcopos* expresses the idea of an overseer. It's easy to see how both might be translated *elder—one who wisely oversees, guides, and counsels.*

The New Testament seems to use *presbyteros* and *episcopos* similarly if not interchangeably. As the early church moved beyond its first-century roots, *episcopos* became "bishop." Bishops became increasingly powerful in the roles of bishops, archbishops, and even popes (the "bishop of Rome"). In addition, some church leaders selfishly vied for ecclesiastical and civic power. The simple overseer of the early church congregation eventually became a formidable political force, battling dukes, nobles, and even emperors.

The original *presbyteros* and *episcopos* didn't have such broad power and authority. Gerhard Kittel's *Theological Dictionary of the New Testament* explains that the meaning of these two words isn't altogether clear (vol. 6, 662). There seemed to be shifts in meaning as the words were used in different places and eras of the New Testament—and even employed by different biblical authors. At times the Bible seems to present both terms as designations of church leaders who resemble the leaders of the synagogues. The apostle Paul, though, refers to the *presbyteroi/episcopoi* in terms of their *functions* in the congregation. They were men to whom the *charisma* (gift of the Spirit) was given. Kittel writes, "Their authority derives from the ministry accepted and discharged by them, not from their status." He adds, "The constitutional principle in the congregation is that of plurality of *charismata* (gifts), not that of a naturally developed tradition which qualifies its bearers and sponsors to lead the church" (664).

Kittel suggests that the authority of the *presbyteroi/episcopoi* in the early church didn't rest on the title, tradition, or vertical positioning of their office. Their leadership roles were rooted in their calling to the ministry, in their ministry work itself, and in the charismatic gifts of the Spirit necessary to fulfill their ministerial role. In the very early congregations, leaders were Spirit-gifted people who were recognized for their gifts and who lovingly oversaw the congregation, giving wisdom and guidance drawn from their faith and maturity.

The idea of church authority defined primarily by position rather than servant wisdom and experience gradually replaced the early church's concept of presbyter. The authority of today's elders, deacons, and bishops often derives from vertical position in church governance, not from their recognized gifts of the Spirit along with a confirmed sense of calling. Often a pastor, in particular, is hired because of their academic accomplishments, preaching and practical ministry skills, and denominational or other ecclesiastical credentials—all of which might be necessary but are insufficient for leadership as defined by Scripture. Such qualifications don't necessarily mean the person is truly gifted as a wise overseer of the congregation.

Addressing Problems with Power and Authority

A range of practical problems can occur in church governance when leaders and members confuse work with service, and power with gifts and calling.

Candidates who don't really want to be elected. A person is invited to become an elder in a congregation. The external call is certainly present. Are the *gifts* and *internal call* present? I remember attending a congregational meeting during my teen years. When paper ballots were passed out for the elder vote, a couple of men sitting by me—whose names were on the ballot— began whispering to others around them, "Don't vote for me." I wondered, "Did these men accept the nomination for elder out of duty and guilt rather than gifts and calling?"

Serving without the necessary gifts. Elders—overseers, bishops, deacons— are asked to do many and diverse things. It's unrealistic to assume that each office holder has the gifts to do everything expected—to teach, discipline, lead committees, administer, make financial decisions, and more. In the vertical system, men and women invariably are asked to do things for which they aren't gifted. The result sometimes is burnout and the lack of congregational passion for volunteerism.

Confusing leadership labels with biblical callings. People act out what their label or title actually says or *what they perceive it to mean.* If the predominant sense of the label "elder" is CEO, executive board member, or trustee, the attitudes and actions of the elders will reflect their perceptions of what these corporate titles mean to them and what the holders of such titles supposedly do. Certainly the church has a business-like side. Clearly having the qualities of an effective CEO could help a pastor perform more effectively as an administrative leader. But the business world does not normally prepare CEOs to be wise and Spirit-filled servants with the characteristics of biblical church leaders. When the role of the church shepherd is understood vertically only as a managerial position in the church, he or she may not adequately shepherd the congregation as organism.

I've seen gifted potential leaders' attitudes and actions shift when elected elder. Once elected, leaders took on a new sense of purpose but focused excessively on bringing their own sense of order and correctness to the congregation. I recall an elected elder who developed a passion for single-handedly purifying the church. He demanded to investigate past minutes of elder meetings. He suspected that previous church-discipline decisions had been too "liberal" and demanded that some previously disciplined congregants be re-examined. He sought to reopen closed cases so the church could be fully cleansed once and for all. Elder meetings became strained debates over legal, moral, and institutional propriety. I've seen other newly-elected elders demand that meetings and the church as a whole mirror formal institutional processes, such as requiring that secretaries take legal minutes, that Robert's Rules of Order be legalistically applied, and that leadership meetings be strictly limited to elders.

Overcoming Excessively Institutional Leadership

One solution to the potential problems of overly institutional leadership and top-down church governance is to anchor the church's volunteerism in gifts, calling, and passion. This can be done in three steps.

STEP ONE
Eliminate the vertical system of authority and institute horizontal governance.

STEP TWO
Discontinue the practice of having just one or two leadership bodies made up exclusively of elders, deacons, presbyters, and trustees. Instead, invite the congregation first to examine and discover its needs. Such needs would include: (1) what the Bible asks of a congregation, (2) the ministry needs and opportunities unique to the congregation, (3) the need to explore a working vision of caring for people within the congregation's own history and current setting, and (4) the need for a mission statement. The church forms leadership groups and identifies individuals to address the most compelling needs (the whats) and define the necessary actions (the hows).

The whats and the hows might include:

- finding older, wiser people to oversee and guide the church and pastor(s)
- identifying people with business gifts who will care for the financial aspects of the church
- determining people with gifts of caring for the sick and needy
- selecting paid and unpaid people with unique gifts to direct common ministries such as youth, evangelism, arts and music, and children
- appointing task forces made up of uniquely gifted people who tackle special challenges that arise—such as building projects, fundraisers, and facilities-usage policies
- calling those people who are gifted in matters relating to the building and grounds to care for and oversee the physical property
- These groups and their leaders will have the trench authority to make decisions and to act as they see fit within the natural boundaries of church policies and peer relationships.

STEP THREE

Change labels. In some congregations, labels such as elder, deacon, presbyter, trustee, and board probably should no longer be used since they carry too much secular and/or historical baggage. If needed, new labels should mirror the gifts, callings, and tasks rather than the positions per se. People will focus on what their label actually means instead of what traditional assumptions and practices have led them to assume it means.

There will still be wise and overseeing "elders" (perhaps with a different label), and they will still "rule," but they will do so in their role of caretaking shepherds rather than managers or executives. These will generally be people who have exhibited gifts of spiritual maturity, love for the Lord and the church, and wisdom in addressing sensitive matters in and outside of the church. Their unique role will be overseeing the spiritual character and life of the church and its pastors, and will have little to do with the institutional side of the church. They will be among those in the congregation whose lives speak love and care.

The church will also have "deacons" (with varying labels). Their work will be divided among gifted individuals and small groups of people who have gifts in the area of business, compassion, caring, and community involvement. Each group or individual will be labeled according to their task and goals in tune with the churches vision and mission statements. They, too, will speak the Gospel by their attitudes and their works.

With this type of horizontal system, the congregational passion can be high and burnout low. The potential of drawing in volunteers increases. In the twenty years I've used this system, no one has ever turned down the invitation to fill the role of what has been traditionally called elder. In fact, when their term is finished they usually don't want to retire or step down. When gifts are freely used with mutual, loving accountability, congregants experience passion and joy.

Discussion Questions

1. Would you be open to different understandings of the words "elder" and "deacon" than the ones currently used in your church—assuming you use them? Does the lack of clarity in New Testament uses of the labels seem to suggest that churches need to define them for their own needs?
2. Are there people in your church who are willing to "run for office" but don't really want to serve? If so, why would they serve? What does your response say about your church's governance?
3. Do your church members seem to change their attitudes and actions when elected to church office—or when graduating from seminary—in tune with leadership stereotypes or labels? Is this necessarily wrong? Explain.
4. Would the leadership ideas in this chapter work in your congregation? If your church is affiliated with a denomination, what would denominational leaders think about your congregation adopting such governance?

20

Renewing Traditional Ministries

The overall goal in church leadership is to bring glory to God by developing a working vision of caring for people. Each church considers its own unique context as it establishes a mission statement that identifies who is served and how they are served. The leaders help inspire and equip diversely gifted and called people to love God, first, and their neighbors as themselves. God is glorified as the church obeys Scripture and cares for people. The church considers people's unique gifts and passionately equips them to joyfully serve others.

The goal in employing horizontal governance isn't just to try a different form of governance. The goal is to pour new wine into new wineskins. In this chapter, I explain how the horizontal governance can work in various congregational ministry contexts.

Creating a Horizontal Governance Model

The place to begin creating a horizontal governance model is with typical ministries such as youth, worship, children, congregational care, and finances. The church seeks congregants (or perhaps those not currently attending the church if paid staff are preferred over volunteers) to lead in each area. Only people with the gifts and calling for each distinct ministry area are considered.

These new directors are basically equal to each other. Ministry directors have the freedom to plan, decide, and execute as they see fit. They don't have to present their everyday ideas and requests to boards or committees. Each leader is subject only to the boundaries of church policy, their individual budget, and the sensitivity of their fellow leaders. Each receives guidance as needed from a pastor or some other wise person working among them.

Each director is responsible for finding their own volunteers. The leader has excitement and passion, making the mood right for volunteers wanting to join. The leaders personally recruit people from the congregation; these are people with the gifts and callings to do the work of that particular ministry. The leader forms the team. The team enjoys the work and the process of the ministry because of the freedom to work in the trench as they have been gifted and called. The team will not be stalled or second-guessed by a bureaucratic structure that doesn't really understand the trench. The team and its leader cast the vision for the ministry, decide how best to achieve the goals, and move ahead, acting as they see fit.

Forming such teams with their directors is the first step. The church then asks what other biblical ministries require teams and directors. Consider each of the following areas.

Organizing Financial and Legal Ministries

Gifts and calling are required to care for the church as an institutional as well as organic congregation. The business side of the church is critically important and requires special stewardship abilities. These weighty matters aren't simply assigned to one group (such as deacons). A team of volunteers who are astute in business and finance are asked to administer and oversee the financial and other business and legal matters of the congregation. Another small group might be formed to oversee the money allotted to benevolence; members exhibit gifts in management and compassion.

Overseeing the Congregation's Spiritual Health

The spiritual oversight of the congregation is the role and responsibility of the older and wiser members. This small group includes three or four people who show love for the church along with the gifts of wisdom and discernment. This group is what has often been labeled "elders." The difference is that the group focuses on the organic nature of the church. The group rarely votes and tends to stay away from business, financial, and legal matters unless wisdom and guidance are requested. The types of things this group does are:

- hold the pastor and other leaders spiritually accountable
- assess the overall work of the pastor and leaders related to the impact of their work on the congregation
- address sensitive personal issues arising within the church leadership and other members
- review and supervise the overall spiritual health and stability of the church
- assist with the sacraments

The group need not meet often, but it must be ready to come together when a pressing issue threatens the security of the church or one of its leaders. Because the group doesn't do the work of the gifted ministry leaders and their ministry teams, there is little or no politics and arm twisting. The mood in the oversight meetings is one of wise people gathering to discuss and guide with mutual accountability. Such an atmosphere keeps the stress low and the commitment level high. People are asked to serve by the pastor and affirmed by the congregation. There is no slate of candidates facing a final vote. People are selected by the pastor based on gifts and calling.

The small group emphasizes shepherding (Ezek. 34). To affirm the shepherding role and to remove the sense of executive power, the label "elder" might be replaced with a name more in tune with the early New Testament concept of *presbyteros* and *episcopos*. At my church, we adopted the label "advisory pastors"—*advisory* because the role is to lead, guide, care, and uplift, and *pastor* because it focuses on shepherding.

But aren't elders supposed to *rule*? Admittedly, using the term advisory pastors doesn't emphasize ruling—at least not in the sense of "running the show." The focus is not on organizational power and executive management. The church's team leader-directors themselves have the freedom to run the activities of their trench. Biblically speaking, however, the shepherd carries the rod as well as the staff. In a horizontal system, there is great peace from day to day, and the gifted and called freely do their work. When, however, there is a moral matter, an unsolvable problem, a wayward leader, a ministry out of control, a staff member who requires termination, the advisory group meets and exerts the rod. They are the court of last appeal and the first to be called when things go awry. After getting tough, making a hard decision, and leading in murky waters, they are happy to lay down the rod and pick up the staff. In fact, they are called and gifted to do so.

Being Hospitable

Hospitality includes calling on people with special needs and caring for those in special situations. A small hospitality group is formed and led by its director. This group sends cards, makes calls at hospitals and funeral homes, brings meals, visits the sick, and provides special attention to new babies and parents. It might be called a "Care Group." If there is sufficient talent and need in the church, this group can also generate other, related ministries, such as "Divorce Care" or "Grief Share" ministries.

Organizing Big Projects

From time to time, church projects go far beyond what the usual leadership groups can handle. Such greater tasks might include building projects, major fundraising drives, complex moral questions facing the church, and the need to review and possibly revise a significant church policy. People with gifts, calling, and passion for the topic are brought together as a team to address the issue, solve the problem, or accomplish the task. A simple label such as "Task Force" is adequate and useful. When the task is completed, the group is disbanded. If the problem is a moral matter or one of major church policy, advisory pastors are involved and may need to rule on the final proposal.

Stewarding Building and Grounds

A leadership team oversees building and grounds. This isn't simply a building committee that does maintenance and makes recommendations to a board. This group actually stewards everything related to building and grounds. It has the same parameters as the other ministries; it is subject to church policies (including budget) and the boundaries of peer accountability. Members run ideas by the pastor(s) and other staff persons when it looks like ideas will impact various ministries. In general, they and the custodian just "do it."

Again, the freedom to exercise trench authority is a marvelous motivator and keeps a gifted team busy, productive, and satisfied over time.

Senior Pastoring

What role should the senior pastor play in the administrative process? In horizontal governance, the pastor becomes the knowledgeable gatekeeper for the church and its leaders. The pastor filters or otherwise handles leadership issues. The senior pastor doesn't solve all the issues that come across their desk, but knows where to direct the congregants and ministry leaders seeking advice; this is the gatekeeper function. This pastor serves as the conduit between paid and volunteer staff and the advisory pastors. As issues come up that are beyond the scope of the staff volunteers, the pastor invites the advisory pastors to consider such issues. The pastor also serves as the shepherd to the shepherds—as shepherd to the staff volunteers and smaller service groups. The senior pastor guides and directs with wisdom and encouragement. The pastor never becomes the sole power person at the top of vertical governance, dictating what others must do. Rather, the pastor as shepherd cares for the flock, primarily alongside the other servants.

A Unique Ministry

The church may encounter an opportunity to embark on a unique working challenge not already within its specific mission statement but in tune with its vision of caring for people. There are many examples: purchasing a camp for camping and retreat ministries; using a storefront ministry to offer clothing, food, and the Gospel to low-income families; visiting and writing to prisoners; setting up a food bank in the church building to serve the neighborhood.

When a special ministry opportunity comes to the attention of advisory pastors or other leaders are staff, the pastor can quickly seek others' advice, inform the advisory pastors and various ministry directors, and decide whether or not to move ahead. If the senior minister decides to proceed and—in appropriate consultation with other directors—finds someone with appropriate gifts and a sense of calling, that person could immediately be put in charge or further equipped with some training or mentoring. As a new ministry director, that called, gifted, and possibly further-equipped person begins building a team of volunteers. The senior pastor and advisors need to discern whether the called leader also feels gifted for the tasks ahead, since external and internal calls are not always identical. If not, another possible leader needs to be called.

A new team and its director have the freedom to vision, experiment, and work within the framework of church policy, budget, and relationships with other team directors. The new team is sent forward with God's blessing to carry the vision and go forth! If the impact of the new ministry eventually seems promising, it would be incorporated into the church's mission statement.

Years ago one of our pastors asked if he could begin having worship on Friday evenings for people with addictions and related problems. The pastor had the gifts, calling, and passion for the work. After conversations with other team ministry leaders and our advisory pastors, we gave the green light and stepped back. Not all new ideas and projects will be successful. Some die a quick death, others slowly. But many do succeed. This one became huge. Twelve years after launching it, the ministry already included two full-time staff and a volunteer team of over seventy persons. The worship and twelve-step groups minister to over two-hundred people every Friday evening throughout the year.

Developing Creative Worship Content

Pastors can grow stale. So can their preaching. Realizing this, one of our staff approached me for permission to begin a new ministry called "Creative Teams." The concept was for teams of volunteers to come together to plan worship service content, including a relevant sermon topic and whatever worship materials could assist in preaching, teaching and developing the topics used during Sunday-morning worship. In spite of the fact that this unusual worship planning approach would limit and potentially direct my preaching options, I thought it was worth a try. For one thing, it meant that I would receive direct congregational input on congregants' felt needs. So I stepped aside and said, "Do it!" Teams were formed and the ministry was launched.

Today, many congregants meet weekly in one of two teams, discussing and planning worship. Of course, I have the authority to trump their decisions, including rejecting a sermon topic—such as their idea that I do a month-long series on sexuality. I have the benefit of working with the team on developing topics and materials—such as a series on marriage which included some material on sexuality. I have found the work of the teams extremely helpful in keeping my preaching fresh and vibrant. The team's ideas challenge me to present deeply biblical material in new and interesting ways (such as preaching on "Mrs. Noah" and "Mrs. Pilate").

Relating across Ministries

Horizontal governance isn't strictly a congregational governance model. The church benefits from a host of relatively independent, Spirit-gifted ministry leaders and volunteers. At times, however, the issues and policies will be so global or sensitive that a decision by the few isn't appropriate. Amendments to church policy, changes in worship times, the hiring of paid staff, the approval of significant budget items, and the creation of new staff positions are examples of situations when the congregation is brought together for discussion and, if necessary, a vote.

The horizontal model requires mutual trust, respect, and cooperation among church staff and other leaders. There is very little committee work and voting. People who feel strongly called and gifted rise up from the congregation to lead. Decisions are made daily by those in the trenches who are closest to the situation and are the best informed and most capable of deciding. Major decisions and disagreements ultimately go to the advisory pastors as well as to the congregation. The pastor and sometimes other called and gifted leaders are gatekeepers, directing inquiries to the best place for follow-up.

Discipline among staff and volunteer leaders is maintained by mutual sharing and respecting each other's boundaries. Matthew 18 provides the system for interpersonal resolution; conflicts are best resolved directly at the interpersonal level. Burnout is low due to minimal politics, mutual accountability, the sense of calling, and the effective use of gifts that produce passion for the work. Volunteerism is high because people know they're needed and that their ideas and decisions are respected. Because implementation of ideas and decisions is swift and efficient, people are able to do what they *love*, and *do* what they love. The church works as an institution without losing its uniqueness as an organism. The church uses leaders well and focuses on caring for the people who are caring for other people. The church is then both biblical and faithful.

Discussion Questions

1. How can a congregation go about developing a horizontal governance structure? Would the processes suggested in this chapter for developing such horizontal governance be adequate for your congregation? If not, how might your church proceed?
2. In the section on spiritual oversight of a congregation, is enough power and authority given to the group? Has the new approach maintained the concept of "rule by elders" (the rod of the shepherd)? Would this approach to oversight be better for your congregation than its present system—if it has one?
3. With the assortment of teams and leaders all "doing their own thing" in horizontal governance, would the resulting dynamism potentially lead to a confusing mess? If so, how might that be prevented in your church?
4. Is innovative church governance possible without risking a mess? Is growth possible without some messy effects? How much mess is necessary? How much is too much?

21

Wisely Risking for the Love of God

Will employing a horizontal governance structure and focusing on caring for people foster theological liberalism or weak discipline within the church? Will it lead to divisions and controversies? Will it even succeed? These are all valid questions. They're honest questions. They deserve forthright answers.

In this final chapter I'd like to focus directly on the value of horizontal governance and congregational empowerment in the living faithfulness of congregations. All forms of church governance have strengths and weaknesses, and every one of them can be abused by leaders with ill intent, undeveloped skills, or a mistaken sense of calling or giftedness. But I hope that by the end of this chapter you'll be inspired by the opportunities for genuine spiritual growth within the organizational parameters I've discussed previously. There are potential risks and benefits. Often the greatest blessings occur when congregations take measured but still challenging risks.

There is no single way of being and doing church. So much of being faithful is about making tough decisions. The biblical idea of Christian freedom is abundantly clear in the New Testament, where the apostle Paul, among others, recognizes that the church will always be simultaneously biblical and cultural (Gal. 5). We followers of Jesus Christ know that we should obediently adhere to all biblical guidance, including the Ten Commandments and the Sermon on the Mount, but we also recognize that we have to apply such guidance to specific cultural contexts. As I pointed out earlier, titles like "elder" and "deacon" were used somewhat differently even among early churches. It seems that God wants us all to work out the implications of our faith in our own situations, congregation by congregation. We have to know and live Scripture by planting it in culture. We must be faithful to our Lord and savior. But we also have to take risks along the way or we may slip into self-righteousness and stop growing in the faith. Abraham went forward in faith even though he didn't know where he was going (Heb. 11:8). How can we do any less?

We have to be very careful that we don't simply fall into the trap of believing that the way we've always done church is necessarily the most biblical or the most effective way of doing it. Early in this book I examined the danger of church traditions "becoming scripture"—of *inscripturating* the church's culture. There is also an opposing threat of destroying precious traditions that God intends for his church, of demolishing distinctly biblical practices that define a faithful church. When the church adopts a working vision of caring for people, it must be sure not to lose its biblical moorings and mandates along the way. We have to discipline ourselves to stay on biblical track even as we innovatively launch new forms of church governance and innovative ways of being faithful congregations. The purpose of congregational change should be to become more creatively and relevantly biblical, not to become more impressively successful.

Consider the central church activities of preaching, worshiping, disciplining, evangelizing, and performing the sacraments. The key in maintaining these as vital practices is looking carefully at what is truly biblical about them and what is only humanly created culture. For example, particular methods of practicing the sacraments may not be biblical even though the sacraments themselves are. The church must always ask how conducting the sacraments truly ministers to people, so that Christ is present and congregants' faithful unity in Christ is nurtured and sustained. Church leaders need to ensure that they know the biblical purpose for the sacraments and that the congregation practices the sacraments in tune with that purpose. Leaders need to ask the same kinds of questions for everything from preaching to evangelism. No particular form of church governance can guarantee such faithful understandings and practice.

Situating Worship

Worship has always been an area of struggle—traditional versus contemporary, formal versus informal, elaborate versus simple, liturgical vs. free-form, and so forth. Again, church leaders need to consider how their congregation best assembles and rightly praises God in spirit and truth. There is little in Scripture telling us specifically how to do church on Sunday. Surely we shouldn't "neglect the gathering of God's people" (Heb. 10:25). But once we gather, the spiritual needs of the people ought to define what happens. When a congregation has a significant number of people who are deeply committed to hymn singing and long, exegetical sermons, the leadership must respond. This could mean having two services, running them close enough together so people see and greet each other as they're coming and going. The key to success in worship is biblical excellence tuned for a specific congregation. No congregation can do all types of worship effectively for all kinds of people. When hymns are sung, the church needs a highly talented musical crew. When contemporary songs are sung, accomplished musicians are essential. Relevance is no excuse for mediocrity, but technical excellence without meaningful relevance is similarly inexcusable.

Contextualizing Preaching

The preaching needs to connect uniquely with the people who gather for each service. Elements of each sermon should reach many parts of a congregation. A solid message should zero in on the gathered group. Whether the group leans toward traditional or contemporary worship, church leaders shouldn't assume that modern audiences want to hear only what they're used to hearing and singing. All congregants want to hear the Word—although some congregants will always be content with a few good stories and words of encouragement. Most want the Word—they want to learn and to grow in the Lord. The style of preaching may change accordingly. Some of the language and illustrations may change, but congregations basically are the same in their need and desire for the Word. The Sunday message could well be the most important activity the pastor performs all week in terms of providing leadership by faithfully serving the needs of people. But all leaders can serve the pastor with helpful feedback, ideas, and materials for future sermons.

Disciplining Wisely

Church discipline is necessary in a truly biblical congregation. Again, however, the working vision demands that discipline follow a biblical standard aimed at caring for those who are giving and receiving discipline—along with those who might hear about it even when it's administered confidentially. But discipline might be carried out differently in various congregations in order to ensure that the church understands the nature and purpose of such discipline. Discipline should never be applied in ways that violate confidentiality or result in ridicule, embarrassment, or shunning. A church with a working vision of caring for people won't practice discipline loosely. The key is whether the person under discipline is clearly violating a nonnegotiable rule of Scripture or is merely violating one of the church's own cultural values. Culture is still important. We need to both avoid offending others and appropriately be all things to all people. But cultural styles and expressions aren't Scripture. Merely offending or disappointing people is not the same as sinning against God and neighbor.

For example, contemporary churches have usually forbidden people living together without a marriage ceremony. We reasonably extrapolate from Scripture that a formal statement of marriage is needed. But no specific biblical passage addresses the topic. Isaac and Rebecca slept in Isaac's mother's tent before they were married. Mary was betrothed to Joseph. What do all the biblical examples of marriage mean?

I'm personally content with the historical understanding that couples should not live together without marriage. But does a young, unwed couple from church, living together, require discipline? If so, what kind of discipline? What if the "guilty" couple extrapolates from Scripture that the body is a temple of the Holy Spirit? (e.g., 1 Cor. 6). Does that apply to unwed sexual relations? Does it also apply to smoking, overeating, and insufficient exercise? What if a church has a tradition of opposing alcohol even though there are biblical passages that abhor drunkenness and others that permit drinking wine in moderation? What do we do with the discipline of those who are lazy and a gossipy? (2 Thes. 3:11). Paul seems to permit the shunning of such talkative freeloaders. These and many other issues can be so difficult for church discipline that some elders and pastors might avoid them. Leaders tend either just to "let it go" or to take a hard line, as if Scripture is either never or always absolutely clear on every subject.

The church needs to carefully define what clearly violates Scripture and what merely opposes particular culture. If some cultural practices oppose Scripture, they demand church action. For example, the couple living together might be removed from any position of leadership but not placed under discipline if they're indeed betrothed and set to wed. The couple may need wise counsel from the pastor or another counselor. But those who gossip about the couple might also require some discipline.

Is the pastor necessarily the best one to approach the topic with the couple? Under horizontal authority, if the young man sings in the choir, perhaps the choir director should speak with the couple—maybe along with the pastor or another leader. Even in matters of discipline, horizontal authority provides closer contact with congregants at the level of congregants' own service in the church. Moreover, horizontal governance makes it clear to the congregation that congregants have mutual accountability to fulfill Jesus' intent that those who have a problem with someone else's conduct should first address the issue with that person themselves (Matt. 18).

If two pastors simply show up at the young couple's door, the couple may be overwhelmed with fear, resentment, and confusion. Instead, a pastor and choir director could form a plan of action and interact in a personal, caring, and pointed way with the couple. The Bible study leader might be the most appropriate one to talk with the gossiper who attends the Bible study—assuming the leader has the needed interpersonal skills. The director of the building and grounds team might be the best one to talk to their team member who shows up late for maintenance work, reeking of alcohol. This is all done in concert with the pastor, who monitors the activities. Individual ministry directors should not address such weighty disciplinary matters on their own without counsel and accountability.

Taking Risks

Another challenge for the church is risk. The church hoping to pour new wine into new wineskins may want to adopt the slogan: "Fearing the risk and risking the fear." The tagline suggests that the church ought to seriously consider taking risks. In considering a risk, there ought to be fear. Real fear. What if things do go haywire? What if we can't handle the changes as they unfold? What if we as a church get hurt? What if we cause brothers and sisters to stumble in their faith? Such fear helps keep the church realistic, humble, and God-fearing so it doesn't foolishly charge into areas that are likely to damage rather than serve people. At the same time, the church needs to take risks. It needs to come to the point of saying, "Okay, let's go! Let's do it. Let's take the risk and see where God leads!"

Risks are evident in a number of church areas, including governance. For instance, we hired a man recently released from prison who had the gifts, talents, and calling needed for one of our ministries. We did this after we had a sad experience with another returning citizen (ex-prisoner) whom we had placed into an important volunteer position. During his time volunteering, he committed another crime and eventually returned to prison for life. It was not easy to inform the congregation. People were hurt, frustrated, and angry with him and with church leaders. Even so, when the opportunity again arose to place a returning citizen into a staff position, we still took the risk. Why? We were convinced we were called and gifted to serve returning citizens.

Each church finds its own level of risk. When a church decides to take a risk, some members will warn, "What if it doesn't work?" Leaders should answer honestly, "You're right! It might not. But even if it doesn't work, we need to take the risk." Leaders and congregations can grow from such risks. Jesus surrounded himself with questioning people. How can we do less? The church learns to live in the context of risk—the tension between great success and dismal failure, between faithfulness and doubt, between wisdom and foolishness, between institution and organism, and so many more tensions. Tension can be very healthy. Church leaders need to be taught and to expect risk even in providing leadership.

In the last chapter I mentioned a staff person who felt called to begin a Friday-evening worship service for addicts and others with deep hurts and difficult problems. That staff member took a huge risk. He put some of his other assignments on hold in order to launch this new ministry with no guarantee of success and with plenty of risk. What if the new ministry failed? Would he still have a job? This was an extremely tense time for me, too, because that staff person was my adult son, our associate pastor. But all I could do—all any of us can do—in such a risky situation was to give the situation to God, bless the gifted and called leader, and turn him loose to serve and to bless.

Reaching Beyond Traditional Sunday Ministry

The church should also think in terms of an active week of ministry rather than just a hectic Sunday. There is something deadening about a church building used only once weekly. Leaders should ask, "How can we make this place a daily hub of neighborhood and congregational activity?" Providing daycare, conducting various Bible studies, offering activities for children and youth, hosting an elderly activity center, establishing a library reading room for the wider community, renting rooms to community groups—all of these and many more are somewhat risky ways that to transform underused church building into a bustling community that engages the outside world as well as serves its own members. When the congregation is active, the community notices and congregants take pride in their building and the neighborhood. Good feelings lead to happy members and a strong core of support.

Form a risky but biblical vision for your church as a place of faithful followers of Jesus Christ who care for others and themselves. Teach the vision to your congregants. Live the vision with them, constantly reminding them of the joy of being a unified body of Christ that glorifies God by faithfully using a variety of people and gifts to care for people. Establish a mission statement that clarifies to whom and how your church is called to minister. In this way, you, too, can taste the sweetness of new wine in new wineskins, the body of Christ pouring itself out in new, biblical, and even delightful ways, according to the gifts given by God's own Spirit, full of passion and joy. Now *that's* how we become recovering churchists who faithfully do church together!

Discussion Questions

1. Should churches take risks—or is it too much like gambling, namely, great if you win but awful if you lose?

2. The chapter calls for a form of discipline in which the task is shared among the various team leaders in the church. That process, based on Matthew 18 (see below), generally moves away from the vertical approach traditionally included in the roles of elders and deacons. Is horizontal governance wise in a church today, even if Matthew 18 seems to suggest it? Explain.

3. If there are disagreements within a congregation over worship styles, is it a good idea to provide multiple worship services for the different groups? Would that keep peace in the church more than developing one blended service to keep members together?

4. Does your reading and discussion of this book lead you to a sense that maybe your church needs refreshment, renewal, and even change? What concepts in the book have given you the most constructive ideas and possible plans for your own church's renewal and growth? Is such change possible in your church? Are you being called to help lead the way?

If your brother or sister sins, go and point out their fault, just between the two of you. If they listen to you, you have won them over. But if they will not listen, take one or two others along, so that 'every matter may be established by the testimony of two or three witnesses.' If they still refuse to listen, tell it to the church; and if they refuse to listen even to the church, treat them as you would a pagan or a tax collector (Matt. 18:15–17).

CPSIA information can be obtained at www.ICGtesting.com
Printed in the USA
BVOW011406161011

273676BV00001B/7/P